Innkeepers' Best

Low-Fat Breakfasts

60 Delicious Recipes Shared by
Bed & Breakfast Innkeepers
Across the Country

Laura Zahn

Down to Earth Publications

Published by
Down to Earth Publications
1032 West Montana Avenue
St. Paul, MN 55117

Library of Congress Cataloging in Publication Data

Zahn, Laura C., 1957-
 Innkeepers' best low-fat breakfasts / Laura C. Zahn
   p. cm.
 Includes index.
 ISBN 0-939301-18-0
 1. Breakfasts. 2. Low-fat cooking. 3. Bed-and-breakfast accommodations— U.S.— directories.
 TX733.Z3

Dewey System - Low-Fat Cooking - 641.5638

Printed in the USA
97 98 99 00 01 5 4 3 2 1

Cover photo of breakfast from the Inn at the Round Barn Farm, Waitsfield, Vermont (recipe page 125), courtesy of the Inn at the Round Barn Farm. Back cover photo courtesy of the Beazley House, Napa, California (recipes on pages 53, 55, and 91). Many thanks to these inns — and the others — all who shared their delicious recipes and wonderful stories!

Cover and interior design by Helene C. J. Anderson, Stillwater, Minnesota.

To order additional copies by mail, send a check or money order for $12.95 each to Down to Earth Publications, 1032 W. Montana Ave., St. Paul, MN 55117 (includes shipping by 4th class mail). If you wish UPS delivery, send a check for $13.95 and include a street address (no P.O. boxes). To charge your order with a Visa or MasterCard, call 800-585-6211 or fax 612-488-7862.

Introduction

*G*reat low-fat breakfasts at elegant country inns and bed-and-breakfasts? How can that be? These are places known for decadent breakfast feasts! More and more travelers are requesting low-fat breakfast fare — and more and more innkeepers are adapting their own diets to cut the fat, at least a little. And nearly all innkeepers will try to accommodate dietary requests if they are made at the time of the reservation. So even if a particular inn is renowned for its sinfully delicious, calorie-laden fare, chances are good that a meal low in fat is easily arranged.

In this book, innkeepers across the country share sixty of their very best recipes. These are the ones that get "ooohs" and "aaahs" from guests every time, the ones that repeat guests request, and the ones that innkeepers are most-often asked to write down so guests can try them at home. Try Creme Caramel Overnight French Toast, Chilled Cantaloupe Soup, Luscious Lemon Pancakes, or Cranberry Orange Scones — just a sampling of the mouthwatering recipes innkeepers have made again and again, and now are sharing with home cooks.

For innkeepers, delicious low-fat fare is very important — building their business means enticing guests to return. A bland breakfast, even if it is healthy, won't help matters. One of the greatest advantages for home cooks is that many innkeepers are home cooks, too — they are working in a B&B kitchen, which is hardly different from a home kitchen. And all inns — even those inns that have chefs — want wonderful recipes that are quick. So many of these sixty recipes are time-savers, as well.

Nancy Danley, owner of the McCallum House in Austin, Texas, is one innkeeper who specializes in great fat-free fare. She offers this advice for "painless" adaptation to fat-free cooking: "I replace oil with unsweetened applesauce one-to-one. I cut back on sugar a bit. Use only egg whites: Throw out the yolks, give them to your cat, or use some, but not all, in the recipe. I often use two egg whites to replace one whole egg. Fat- and cholesterol-free egg substitutes are fine, but more expensive than my method." She also notes that muffins, cakes, and pastries should not be overmixed nor overbaked: "Low-fat baked goods are easily dried out." As with other low-fat cooking, taste is important: "Orange zest and a generous use of prescribed spices are good ways to assure plenty of flavor."

Some of these recipes are by innkeepers like Nancy who specialize in serving low-fat foods, and some are by innkeepers who serve it upon request. Some are virtually fat-free, some have lowered amounts of fat, but most are in between. All are by innkeepers who have tried these recipes over and over, and who believe you will love them as much as their guests! Bring a B&B breakfast home today!

— *Laura Zahn*

CONTENTS

Beverages ■ 6 to 13

Fruit ■ 14 to 37

Entrées ■ 38 to 81

Breads and Coffeecakes ■ 82 to 91

Muffins and Scones ■ 92 to 115

Additional Treats ■ 116 to 125

List of Inns by State ■ 126

The Bernerhof Inn

*I*n the late 1800s, travelers heading north through Crawford Notch needed a place to stay in the remote New Hampshire wilderness, so a local businessman built Pleasant Valley Hall. One hundred years later, the inn has been enlarged and improved, but the inn's mission is the same: to provide hospitality to White Mountain travelers.

Ted Wroblewski first saw this inn in 1977, when he and his wife, Sharon, were living in New York City. He went back and told her about it, and they agreed to move here when their oldest child, Brooke, was only six months old. Since then, they've had three more children, all of whom were raised at the inn and worked here at one time or another.

In between its origin and the Wroblewski's ownership, the Bernerhof had been termed Pleasant Valley Farm and Glenwood on the Saco under previous owners. Following World War II, new restaurateurs featured fine Swiss cuisine and changed the name to the House of Bern, named after a region in Switzerland.

Ted and Sharon have completely remodeled the inn at least twice since their ownership, and now the nine rooms are decorated in antiques, some with whirlpool tubs. The inn's restaurant and European-style taproom, the Black Bear Pub, are well-known to White Mountain travelers and residents alike. "A Taste of the Mountains" cooking school is presented at the inn three times a year.

The Bernerhof Inn
Route 302
P.O. Box 240
Glen, NH 03838
603-383-9131
Fax 603-383-0809

Cantaloupe Cooler

At the Bernerhof, guests often choose a high-energy, low-fat beverage to fortify them for a day of skiing or hiking in the White Mountains. This is a perfect summer refresher. Makes 2 servings.

 1 cup diced cantaloupe
 ½ cup yogurt
 2 teaspoons honey
 1 teaspoon lemon juice
 ½ teaspoon grated lemon peel
   thin lemon slices and fresh mint leaves for garnish

- Combine cantaloupe, yogurt, honey, lemon juice, and grated lemon peel in a blender and purée until smooth.
- Pour into chilled glasses, and garnish with lemon slices and mint leaves.

The Rosewood Country Inn

*L*esley and Dick Marquis left high-stress jobs in the city to open a bed-and-breakfast and see their two high-school-age daughters through school. What they found is a picture-perfect country road, along which their inn rests on 12 peaceful acres.

Their life is far different from life in the big city, but the inn itself has required as much work as any full-time (and then some) job. "I had to look at it three times" before she'd agree to buy it, Lesley said, since the inn was too big and needed too much work for what she'd originally envisioned. Now, after months of renovation, restoration, and redecorating, she and Dick are glad to have the extra space to expand their successful business, if they choose.

The inn's seven guestrooms often are filled with mothers and daughters on a special Mother and Daughter Weekend, or couples and friends attending a Weekend Getaways for Gourmet Cooks. Lesley and Dick also offer special packages for lovers and downhill skiers, and they encourage cross-country skiers to enjoy nearby trails.

Lesley's three-course candlelit breakfast is often served fireside or on one of the inn's sunlit porches. On Sunday evenings, the inn is open to the public for elegant desserts and specialty coffees.

The Rosewood Country Inn
67 Pleasant View Road
Bradford, NH 03221
603-938-5253

Citrus Frost

"Tropical Blend and Citrus Frost are great! They're really appreciated by our 'no coffee or tea' guests," says Innkeeper Leslie Marquis. Makes 6 to 8 servings.

2 8-ounce cartons lemon low-fat yogurt
2 cups skim milk
1 6-ounces can frozen orange juice concentrate
ice cubes

- In a blender jar, combine yogurt, milk, and orange juice concentrate. Blend until smooth.
- Refrigerate until ready to serve. Stir before serving. Serve over ice.

Tropical Blend

Makes 4 servings.

2 cups vanilla low-fat yogurt
16 ounces crushed pineapple in juice, undrained
1 cup orange juice
2 ripe kiwi fruit, peeled and sliced
2 tablespoons wheat germ
ice cubes

- Combine yogurt, crushed pineapple and juice, orange juice, kiwi, and wheat germ in blender. Cover and blend on high speed until smooth. Serve immediately over ice.

The Inn on South Street

*G*uests of this stately two-hundred-year-old mansion might enjoy this break-fast beverage in the second-floor country kitchen, overlooking the river and the ocean. Breakfast is made and served there by Eva and Jack Downs, who turned their spacious home into an inn after their children had been raised here.

Eva, formerly an occupational therapist and child care administrator, and Jack, an American history professor, love treating guests to their home and town. Built in the Greek Revival style, the home was moved long ago to this location by teams of oxen. After completely redecorating their home of almost thirty years, the Downses opened four guestrooms, one of which is an apartment suite. The herb and "secret" gardens are exquisite and worth a visit by guests.

The inn is located in Kennebunkport's quiet historic area and is listed on the National Register of Historic Places. Guests can walk down tree-lined streets to restaurants, shops, and the ocean, or take a short drive to golf courses, tennis courts, nature preserves, and wonderful beaches.

The Inn on South Street
P.O. Box 478A
Kennebunkport, ME 04046
207-967-5151
Toll-free 800-963-5151

Minted Watermelon Refresher

Innkeeper Eva Downs serves this with breakfast on hot summer days. She notes it is also very refreshing in the afternoon or evening, perhaps served in the garden or on the porch. Makes about 10 to 12 servings.

$\frac{1}{2}$ watermelon, seeds removed
$\frac{3}{4}$ cup fresh mint leaves
$\frac{1}{2}$ cup frozen orange juice concentrate
  juice of 1 lime
3 to 4 cups ice cubes
  extra lime slices or mint leaves for garnish

- Blend the watermelon, mint leaves, orange juice concentrate, and lime juice, and let stand overnight to blend flavors.
- When ready to serve, crush ice cubes, and add them to the drink. Stir well, and serve in large goblets, garnished with lime slices or mint leaves.

Grant Corner Inn

*B*reakfast is such a special event at Santa Fe's Grant Corner Inn that it is open to the public by reservation. Innkeeper Louise Stewart has earned a great reputation for the inn's food, as well as the 12 guestrooms. How good is breakfast? So good that Louise's Grant Corner Inn cookbook is a best seller among guests who want to take a breakfast home with them!

Louise was born into an innkeeping family, and she's continued the tradition, raising her daughter, "Bumpy," at the inn. Louise's husband, Pat Walter, transformed a three-story Colonial home, right in downtown Santa Fe, into a romantic inn, complete with white picket fence and gazebo. It took nine long months of major renovation before the inn opened in 1982.

The home was built for the Winsor family, whose photo, among others of the home's residents over the years, hangs in the hallway. The dining rooms and parlor are on the first floor, with guestrooms on the second and third floors. The decor includes Louise's collection of antiques, Indian art, and bunnies (every type except the live kind), which have multiplied wildly and are everywhere, from tea pots and napkin rings to door stops.

Grant Corner Inn

122 Grant Avenue
Santa Fe, NM 87501
505-983-6678

Raspberry Fizz

At the Grant Corner Inn, breakfast always begins with some special beverage, perhaps a fruit frappé, or this dairy-free treat. This beverage is tasty, nourishing, and spectacular when presented in a frosted goblet and garnished with lime slices. Makes 2 servings.

  ½ cup fresh or frozen unsweetened raspberries
  ½ cup apricot nectar, chilled
  5 ice cubes
  1 tablespoon powdered sugar
  ½ teaspoon lemon juice
  ¼ cup club soda, chilled
    lime slices for garnish

- Blend raspberries, apricot nectar, and ice on high until smooth.
- Add powdered sugar and lemon juice and blend another 30 seconds. Stir in club soda.
- Pour into frosted, stemmed goblets and garnish with slices of lime.

Healdsburg Inn on the Plaza

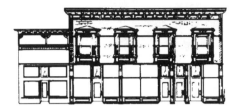

*T*he Healdsburg Inn on the Plaza has the charming distinction of being a 1900 Wells Fargo Building that has been totally renovated into a ten-room bed-and-breakfast hotel. The inn has all the modern conveniences with all the historic charm.

Guests will enjoy browsing through the gift shops and art gallery on the main floor. A grand staircase in the gallery leads to the guest suites, some with baths for two, and some with fireplaces. Each guest suite is furnished in American antiques and decorated in sunrise and sunset colors of peach, rose, and coral.

Daily fare at the Healdsburg Inn on the Plaza includes a wine tasting, a fitting attraction because the inn is located north of San Francisco on Highway 101, right in the center of the Napa, Sonoma, and Mendocino wine region.

A breakfast buffet features cereals, yogurt, fruit juice, coffee and tea, breads, jams and jellies, various breakfast entrées, and fresh fruits. The solarium and roof garden provide a charming common area for guests to meet for coffee, tea, and cakes every afternoon and a full breakfast in the morning.

Healdsburg Inn on the Plaza
110 Matheson Street
Healdsburg, CA 95448
707-433-6991
Fax 707-433-9513

Autumn Fruit Compote

During the colder months when fresh fruit it not at its best even in California, this is a delightful dish to serve. "The touch of Essensia, a sweet dessert wine, adds a wonderful aroma to summon guests to coffee and breakfast," says Innkeeper Trish Hawk. Breakfast is served buffet style in the solarium, where guests may enjoy classical music and the comfort of the fireplace while reading the morning paper. Makes 12 to 15 servings.

2 to 3 cups fresh-squeezed orange juice
   1 8-ounce package dried apricots
   1 8-ounce package dried pears
   1 8-ounce package dried peaches
   1 8-ounce package dried apples
   4 ounces prunes, pitted
   4 ounces dried cherries
  ½ cup fresh or canned chopped pineapple in light syrup
  ½ cup walnuts, optional
   2 cinnamon sticks
   2 ounces Essensia wine
  ¼ cup sweetened coconut for garnish
     mint leaves for garnish

- Combine orange juice, dried apricots, dried pears, dried peaches, dried apples, prunes, dried cherries, pineapple, and walnuts in a 2-quart saucepan. Simmer on low until heated.
- Add cinnamon sticks and Essensia. Simmer on low for 20 to 30 minutes.
- Garnish with sweet coconut and mint leaves. Serve in a chafing dish to keep warm and aromatic.

Window on the Winds
Bed & Breakfast

*L*eanne McClain's two-story log home is the perfect base for a Wyoming vacation. The second floor, with four guestrooms featuring lodgepole pine beds, is reserved for guests. A view of the Wind River Mountains from the fireside gathering room has been known to take more than one guest's breath away.

Leanne is an archeologist who enjoys sharing her perspective on the area and can offer information about the history of the Green River Basin and the Wind River Range. She is also happy to help guests plan their fishing, rafting, riding, skiing, or hiking adventures.

Window on the Winds is located directly on the Continental Divide Snowmobile Trail at elevation 7,175 feet. A guided inn-to-inn snowmobile tour that leads into Yellowstone National Park leaves right from the property. A Wyoming Winter Adventure includes dog sled and sleigh rides, cross-country skiing, and a day of snowmobiling.

Whatever the season, guests can return from a day of outdoor adventure to relax and enjoy the hot tub. Fresh fruits, vegetables and whole grains are always on the breakfast menu. Leanne specializes in western hospitality, even offering to board guests' horses. The bed-and-breakfast is within a two-hour drive of Jackson Hole and the Grand Teton and Yellowstone National Parks.

Window on the Winds
Bed & Breakfast
10151 Highway 191, P.O. Box 996
Pinedale, WY 82941
307-367-2600
Fax 307-367-2395

Baked Apples

This dish takes a little time to prepare, but guests appreciate its flavor, nutrition, and aroma, especially on a winter morning. Leanne McClain's guests are often off to ski or snowmobile after breakfast. She serves these with Scottish Porridge, and has brown sugar, raisins, walnuts, and skim milk on the table. Makes 4 servings.

      4 apples
         nonstick cooking spray, butter flavor
    $\frac{1}{2}$ cup sugar
      2 tablespoons flour
      2 tablespoons wheat germ
  $1\frac{1}{2}$ teaspoon cinnamon
    $\frac{1}{3}$ cup raisins
      8 tablespoons apple juice

- Preheat oven to 350 degrees.
- Core apples. Place in apple bakers or oven-proof bowls. Spray apples with nonstick cooking spray.
- In a separate bowl, mix sugar, flour, wheat germ, and cinnamon. Sprinkle mixture evenly over apples.
- Drop raisins evenly around apples. Pour 2 tablespoons apple juice over each apple.
- Bake at 350 degrees for 35 minutes or until apples are soft (depending on size of apple).

Howard Creek Ranch Inn

*H*oward Creek Ranch is alive with the rural splendor of sweeping ocean and mountain views, forty acres of peace and beauty on the beach near the "Lost Coast," a sixty-mile-long wilderness. The ranch was settled in 1867 as a land grant of thousands of acres, which included a sheep and cattle ranch and a blacksmith shop. Horses, cows, sheep, and llama graze the pastures. The buildings are constructed from virgin redwood from the ranch forest. In the middle of wide green lawns sits a large 1871 farmhouse filled with antiques. A 75-foot swinging bridge spans Howard Creek as it flows past barns and cabins to the beach two hundred yards away. Breakfast is a hearty farm meal with fresh juice, omelets, baked apples with granola, and delicious entrées. The menus change daily.

The Ranch, nominated to the National Historic Register and run by Innkeepers Charles and Sally Grigg, features rooms, suites, and cabins; large comfortable beds with handmade quilts; private decks and balconies; views of the ocean, mountains, or creek; direct access to a long sandy beach with tidepools at low tide and whale watching during migration; prize-winning flower gardens; and much more. *California Magazine* wrote, "Of the dozen or so inns on the West Coast we have visited, this is easily the most enchanting one . . . a private theme park of rural pleasures."

Howard Creek Ranch Inn
40501 North Highway One
P.O. Box 121
Westport, CA 95488
707-964-6725
Fax 707-964-1603

Baked Apples with Granola

These healthy baked apples are part of a nutritious ranch breakfast served at this rural retreat. Makes 8 servings.

4 large Red Rome apples, washed, cored, and halved
2 cups low-fat granola (see Lower-Fat Granola recipe from the Weare-House, page 123)
1 tablespoon, or less, margarine
1 cup nonfat vanilla yogurt
   edible flowers for garnish

- Preheat oven to 350 degrees.
- Place halved and cored apples in a shallow baking dish. (The apples should have a fairly large hole cut out of them in the center.) Fill the holes in the halved apples with the granola. Place $\frac{1}{8}$ tablespoon (or less) of margarine on top of the granola.
- Bake at 350 degrees for 1 hour. Remove the apples from the oven and serve in individual bowls topped with yogurt, or place the apples on a serving tray with each apple dabbed with yogurt. Arrange edible flowers around apples. Serve while hot.

The Inn at Maplewood Farm

*L*aura and Jayme Simoes left busy lives working in a metropolitan public relations firm for life literally along a slow lane. They purchased this bucolic, picture-perfect New England farmhouse and entered careers as innkeepers. Their inn, which has welcomed visitors for two hundred years, sits back from a winding country road, just a short drive from the town of Hillsborough. Located on fourteen acres, guests looking for a quiet getaway are delighted to find the nearest neighbors are a few cows and the 1,400-acre Fox State Forest.

Laura, who also has a food-writing background, prepares dynamite breakfasts, served in the sunny dining room downstairs. While enjoying the fireplace or rocking on the porch are the chosen daytime pursuits of many guests, there is plenty to do in the area. Laura and Jayme love directing guests to little-known antique stores, historic villages, picnic spots and waterfalls, all within a few minutes' drive.

The Inn's four guestrooms are decorated in antiques, including an antique radio at bedside in each. Jayme's infatuation with the Golden Age of Radio has led to his own transmitter on the farm, from which he broadcasts old-time radio programs to the guestrooms via the vintage radios. Request a favorite and, chances are, he's got it in this 1,000-plus show collection.

The Inn at Maplewood Farm

P.O. Box 1478
447 Center Road
Hillsborough, NH 03224
603-464-4242
Toll-free 800-644-6695

Chilled Cantaloupe Soup

For a variation, fresh strawberries can be added to make Strawberry Cantaloupe Soup.
This soup looks pretty in glass bowls or antique bouillon cups, as it is served at the Inn at
Maplewood Farm. Makes 4 servings.

> 1 cantaloupe, peeled, seeded, and coarsely chopped
> 1 cup orange juice
> ½ cup nonfat vanilla yogurt
>   sprigs of fresh mint or edible flowers for garnish

■ In a blender, blend cantaloupe, orange juice, and yogurt until smooth. Serve
   chilled with edible flowers or fresh mint floating on top.

Stonecrest Farm
Bed & Breakfast

*S*ituated on two acres with handsome red barns and lovely old trees, Stonecrest Farm was founded as a dairy farm in 1810 and owned by the Stone family until 1967. Although the farm ceased operation about mid-century, Arthur Stone, an engineer and prominent local citizen, entertained guests such as President Calvin Coolidge and Amelia Earhart in this spacious private home.

Located 3.7 miles south of Dartmouth College in the small village of Wilder, Vermont, near the Connecticut River, Stonecrest Farm is within an easy drive of several major ski and recreation areas. While the majority of Stonecrest's guests are Dartmouth parents, alumni, and visitors, Innkeeper Gail Sanderson welcomes vacationers and businesspeople from many states and foreign countries.

A large formal living room, with a beamed ceiling and a curved staircase, features a wood stove to ward off cold nights. In warmer weather, French doors open to a private stone terrace surrounded by flowers. Stonecrest offers six guestrooms, most with queen beds, down comforters, quilts, abundant books, antiques throughout, and a baby grand piano in the living room.

The varied breakfast menu might offer fresh fruit, juice, homemade breads, muffins or scones, vegetable fritatta, orange French toast, berry pancakes with Vermont maple syrup, or a ricotta- and herb-filled omelet with red pepper sauce.

Stonecrest Farm
Bed & Breakfast
P.O. Box 504
Wilder, VT 05088
802-296-2425
Fax 802-295-1135

Fruit Kabobs with Lemon Ginger Cream

Creative and beautiful cuisine is a hallmark of Stonecrest Farm, and this is a prime example. Innkeeper Gail Sanderson doesn't use any old plain fruit bowl — this dish is served with style. Fruit Kabobs will impress your guests for any meal. Makes 12 kabobs.

½ pineapple, peeled and cored
3 kiwi
12 large strawberries
½ melon
12 skewers

Lemon Ginger Cream
1 cup low-fat sour cream
3 to 4 tablespoons sugar
1 tablespoon lemon juice
1 teaspoon lemon zest
1 tablespoon chopped ginger
fresh mint for garnish

■ Cut pineapple into 12 chunks. Peel kiwi and quarter. Stem strawberries. Peel and cut melon into 12 chunks. Skewer the fruit (1 piece per skewer).
■ To make Lemon Ginger Cream, in a small bowl, combine sour cream, sugar, lemon juice, lemon zest, and ginger. Mix well.
■ Serve skewers on a platter with a garnish of mint and a bowl of Lemon Ginger Cream.

The Parsonage 1908

*F*rom 1908 until the early 1970s, this American Four Square house was home to seven ministers and their families who served one of Holland's early Dutch churches. "The church took excellent care of the Parsonage over the years," said Innkeeper Bonnie McVoy-Verwys, and the oak woodwork, pocket doors, and stairway are still in their original condition. Bonnie has decorated all of it — including the closets — by scouring antique shops for the many interesting pieces that decorate the rooms.

"When I bought this house in 1974, I worked as a supervisor in a sheltered workshop with the adult handicapped, and I had no idea that I would open Holland's first bed-and-breakfast in 1984," she said. She was raising three children alone, and then lost her job. She wanted to work for herself, and since then she's also modeled for local companies, designed bed-and-breakfast flags, and won a silver medal in the Michigan Senior Olympics in tennis doubles.

The Parsonage 1908 is located three minutes away from Hope College. Holland also has Tulip Time in May, Lake Michigan beaches, swimming, golf, antiquing, summer theater, fall colors, cross-country skiing, and fine dining. Saugatuck Resort is only 12 miles away.

The Parsonage 1908
6 East 24th Street
Holland, MI 49423
616-396-1316

Honey Baked Apples

Lower Michigan is apple country, and Innkeeper Bonnie McVoy-Verwys takes advantage of the regional fruit for a low-fat breakfast treat. Makes 4 servings.

4   baking apples
⅛   cup honey
¼   cup water
½   teaspoon lemon rind, grated, or lemon juice

- Preheat oven to 375 degrees.
- Wash and core apples and place them in a baking dish.
- Combine the honey with the water and grated rind or lemon juice. Pour over the apples and bake at 375 degrees, covered, for 30 minutes, basting every 10 minutes.
- Uncover, baste again, and bake 15 additional minutes or until tender.

Lord Mayor's Bed & Breakfast Inn

*T*his elegant Edwardian house was the home of the first mayor of Long Beach, Charles H. Windham. His unofficial Edwardian-style title, Lord Mayor, was bestowed by British beauty contestants enjoying the amenities of this seaside resort in the mid-1900s. The Lord Mayor's house was meticulously restored by historians Reuben and Laura Brasser and received the prestigious 1992 Great American Home Award from the National Trust for Historic Preservation for sensitivity in restoration of a historic house.

Located in the heart of Long Beach, Lord Mayor's Inn is close to many major businesses, shopping, dining, and leisure activities. Within walking distance are city and state government offices, the World Trade Center, the Promenade, Farmers Market, and the Blue Line rapid transit.

Gracious hospitality awaits guests in the Brassers' home. These innkeepers have a reputation for friendliness and fabulous food. Enjoy coffee in the kitchen, a scrumptious breakfast in the dining room or outdoors in the fresh sea air on one of the porches.

There are five spacious bedrooms upstairs. All bedrooms have access to a sun deck. The bedrooms' decors differ, as do the beds. Try the Eastlake Room decorated in Eastlake Design; the four-poster bed in Beppe's Room; the Hawaiian Room with its hand-carved bed; the original master bedroom with its own fireplace; or the room that was originally used by Mayor Windham's daughter, with its twin eighteenth-century Austrian beds.

Lord Mayor's Bed & Breakfast Inn
435 Cedar Avenue
Long Beach, CA 90802
310-436-0324

Mango Delight

"This wonderful recipe is very adaptable to a variety of entrées," wrote Innkeeper Laura Brasser. "Since finding it, we have used it as a summertime side dish for buffet serving or have presented it to guests on individual plates. Mango Delight keeps quite well and guests enjoy it. A delicious variation is to use half bananas and half mangoes." Makes up to 15 servings.

1 cup orange juice
3 packets unflavored gelatin
5 medium, very ripe mangoes
1 cup sugar
1 cup evaporated skim milk
2 cups light whipped topping
   fresh fruit for garnish

- Put the orange juice into a small, heat-proof bowl and sprinkle the gelatin over it. Set aside for 5 minutes.
- Peel mangoes. Cut fruit from pits and purée in a blender or food processor. You should have 4 cups of purée. Transfer the purée into a large mixing bowl and stir in the sugar and evaporated milk.
- Warm the juice and gelatin over a bowl of hot water until liquid and smooth. Whisk the gelatin into the mango mixture.
- Stir in the whipped topping.
- Fill a 10-cup mold with cold water, then pour all the water out. Fill the mold with the mango mixture, cover with plastic wrap, and refrigerate until set, at least 2 to 3 hours.
- To serve: Wrap a warm, damp towel around the mold. Invert a serving plate over the mold and, holding the plate and mold together, turn the plate upright. Lift the mold away carefully. Garnish with fresh fruit. Serve cold.

Apple Gate Bed & Breakfast

*S*easonal fresh fruit is always a part of breakfast at the Apple Gate, and that includes fresh berries from a neighbor's organic farm, as well as apples, of course. Because Apple Gate is located just across the street from a ninety-acre apple orchard, Innkeeper Dianne Legenhausen chose an apple motif to decorate the inn, including naming the four guestrooms after apple varieties. Even Dianne and Ken's one hundred-pound yellow lab, Mac, is named after the McIntosh apple (the cat, Jessie, however, was acquired before the inn and has no apple ties).

Before innkeeping, Dianne taught music to elementary-age children and Ken was a police officer specializing in emergency rescues. While they had many friends in Long Island, New York, where they lived and worked for many years, they decided to head for the Monadnock region of New Hampshire, said to be picture-perfect Currier and Ives country, for their second careers as innkeepers.

They found this 1832 Colonial home just two miles from downtown Peterborough. It offered spacious accommodations for guests, including a double parlor, where guests may enjoy a fire, the library or a TV and collection of videos. Peterborough is home to the Sharon Arts Center and the Legenhausen's bed-and-breakfast is just a few miles from the Temple Mountain and Windblown ski areas.

Apple Gate Bed & Breakfast
199 Upland Road
Peterborough, NH 03458
603-924-6543

Peach Melba

Because Innkeeper Dianne Legenhausen loves Peach Melba, she often ordered it for dessert when she found it on a menu. But it rarely matched her expectations, so she created her own recipe. She serves this dish as a first course for breakfast, using her collection of antique ruby red Depression Glass dessert bowls. Makes 6 servings.

  1 12-ounce package frozen raspberries
  1 10-ounce jar currant jelly
  2 tablespoons sugar
1½ teaspoons cornstarch
  1 tablespoon cold water
  6 canned or fresh peach halves (or melon)
  1 scoop vanilla frozen yogurt (or light ice cream)

- Place the raspberries in a saucepan to thaw.
- Mash the berries with a spoon, and add jelly and sugar. Bring to a boil over low heat.
- Mix the cornstarch and water. Stir into raspberry mixture and bring to a boil again, stirring constantly until clear. Strain and cool sauce.
- Place a peach half in six individual dessert dishes ("Use ruby red dishes — it looks great!"). Top each with a scoop of frozen yogurt. Pour the cooled sauce over the top.

The Inn at Maplewood Farm

*L*aura and Jayme Simoes left busy lives working in a metropolitan public relations firm for life literally along a slow lane. They purchased this bucolic, picture-perfect New England farmhouse and entered careers as innkeepers. Their inn, which has welcomed visitors for two hundred years, sits back from a winding country road, just a short drive from the town of Hillsborough. Located on fourteen acres, guests looking for a quiet getaway are delighted to find the nearest neighbors are a few cows and the 1,400-acre Fox State Forest.

Laura, who also has a food-writing background, prepares dynamite breakfasts, served in the sunny dining room downstairs. While enjoying the fireplace or rocking on the porch are the chosen daytime pursuits of many guests, there is plenty to do in the area. Laura and Jayme love directing guests to little-known antique stores, historic villages, picnic spots and waterfalls, all within a few minutes' drive.

The Inn's four guestrooms are decorated in antiques, including an antique radio at bedside in each. Jayme's infatuation with the Golden Age of Radio has led to his own transmitter on the farm, from which he broadcasts old-time radio programs to the guestrooms via the vintage radios. Request a favorite and, chances are, he's got it in this 1,000-plus show collection.

The Inn at Maplewood Farm

P.O. Box 1478
447 Center Road
Hillsborough, NH 03224
603-464-4242
Toll-free 800-644-6695

Poached Pears

"Our neighbors have pear orchards and someone usually turns up in the fall with a bushel and a smile," says Innkeeper Laura Simoes. "We adore local pears, and this is an easy way to use them up fast. These can also be served chilled on those warm Indian Summer days we seem to get in late September and October." Makes 4 to 6 servings.

1 ½ cups water (or enough to cover pears)
  1 cup dry red wine
  4 whole cloves
  1 cinnamon stick
  1 teaspoon vanilla extract
  ¼ cup all-fruit raspberry or strawberry jam
    lemon zest from ½ or 1 whole lemon
4 to 6 medium pears
    sprinkling of freshly grated nutmeg to top each serving

- Combine water, red wine, cloves, cinnamon stick, vanilla, jam, and lemon zest in a large saucepan. Bring liquid to a boil and cook over high heat for 15 minutes.
- Meanwhile, peel pears, leaving stem intact and removing blossom end (optional: insert a clove in each blossom end). Reduce heat to a simmer. Add pears to saucepan, cover, and poach pears in mixture for 15 minutes or until tender.
- Remove pan from heat and let pears cool in the liquid. Serve warm or chilled with a little extra liquid spooned over each and a grating of fresh nutmeg.

The Hidden Inn

*S*urrounded by wooded acres and nestled in historic Orange, Virginia, the Hidden Inn recreates the charm of a bygone era. The structure was built as a private family home around 1880 by a descendant of Thomas Jefferson, and it is now a romantic, intimate country bed-and-breakfast inn — operating as an inn since 1985. Three buildings have been added to the eight acres, bringing the guestroom total to ten. Four of the rooms have special features such as double-sized whirlpool tubs.

A favorite nearby destination for guests is Monticello, Jefferson's home in Charlottesville; the trip through the beautiful rolling countryside offers stops for antique-shopping, several excellent wineries, and Civil War sites and events during certain times of the year.

Ray (also the town's mayor) and Barbara Lonick are the innkeepers, and will make their guests' visits to the Hidden Inn special. Here travelers will find excellent food, a cozy, comfortable room, and warm, generous hospitality.

The Hidden Inn
249 Caroline Street
Orange, VA 22960
703-672-3625

Poached Winter Fruit

This makes a nice breakfast fruit dish to serve in cooler weather. And it couldn't be easier! Makes 8 to 10 servings.

>   2 8-ounce packages mixed dried fruit
>   4 cups apple juice
>   2 whole cinnamon sticks
>   low-fat sour cream to taste, optional

- Place dried fruit in a saucepan and pour apple juice over to cover the fruit. Add cinnamon sticks and soak overnight.
- In the morning, simmer 10 to 15 minutes on low heat. Serve warm with a dollop of low-fat sour cream, if desired.

Peppertrees Bed & Breakfast Inn

*M*arjorie Martin's yard in Tucson is blessed with two large pepper trees, believed to be as old as her 1905 brick house, and after which her bed-and-breakfast is named. (She also has a lemon tree providing "lemons the size of grapefruit!")

A native of England, Marjorie has decorated her inn with family antiques brought from Britain, and many of her breakfast dishes are old family favorites with an English flavor. She cooks Southwest Tex-Mex cuisine, too, and her creations are so popular she has penned two editions of a Peppertrees cookbook.

Originally, this house had three rooms, a dirt cellar, a back porch for cooking, and an outhouse. It was designed with high ceilings to catch the breezes, and at the time, most Arizonans did their cooking, bathing, and sleeping outside when it was really hot.

Over the years, many additions to the house were made. When Marjorie decided to open it as a B&B, everything was redecorated and a few more additions were made, including a fountain and surrounding patio and garden, where breakfast might be served and where there is always some type of plant in bloom, year-round. Guests at this B&B are only two blocks from the University of Arizona.

Peppertrees Bed & Breakfast Inn
724 East University Boulevard
Tucson, AZ 85719
602-622-7167

Popover Fruit Pie

Innkeeper Marjorie Martin has found that this is an eye-popping way for her guests to enjoy their fruit and yogurt. It's typical of the creative cooking in which she specializes at Peppertrees! Makes 8 servings.

        2 cups plain, nonfat yogurt
2 or 3 tablespoons powdered sugar
        2 tablespoons margarine, melted
        3 eggs, beaten, or equivalent egg substitute
    1½ cups skim milk
     ¾ cup flour
     ⅓ cup sugar
     ½ teaspoon salt
        3 cups strawberries (or other fruit), sliced

- The day before making the pie, put the nonfat yogurt in a sieve lined with 2 layers of cheese cloth. Let the yogurt stand and drain overnight in the refrigerator.
- The next day, put the drained yogurt in a bowl and mix with the powdered sugar. Set aside.
- Preheat the oven to 375 degrees.
- Pour the melted margarine into a pie dish and keep warm in the oven while assembling all the other ingredients.
- Blend or beat well the eggs and the milk. Continue blending and add in the flour, sugar, and salt.
- Pour into the warm pie pan and bake for 30 minutes until the sides are puffed up and golden.
- When the pie has cooled, slightly fill with the yogurt mix and top with sliced strawberries. Serve either warm or cold.

The Inn at 410 Bed & Breakfast

"The place with the personal touch," the Inn at 410 offers four seasons of hospitality. A scrumptious gourmet breakfast is served in Innkeepers Howard and Sally Krueger's dining room each morning; the aroma of home-baked cookies greets guests at the end of their daily excursions.

Ideally located just blocks from historic downtown Flagstaff, the Inn at 410 can serve as a home base for a northern Arizona getaway. Many restaurants, cafes, shops, and galleries are within walking distance of the inn. Day trip destinations from the inn include Grand Canyon National Park, Sedona and Oak Creek Canyon, and the Painted Desert and Petrified Forest.

The inn has nine distinctive suites. Several have private entrances, fireplaces, or whirlpools. One suite is accessible to wheelchairs.

In the dining room, guests are served a full breakfast that features low-fat, low-cholesterol recipes. The inn's spacious parlor, trimmed with oak and furnished with antiques, is a relaxing place to sip hot cider and curl up with a book in front of the fireplace. The gazebo, surrounded by perennial gardens, offers summer guests an intimate retreat for afternoon iced tea.

The Inn at 410 Bed & Breakfast

410 North Leroux Street
Flagstaff, AZ 86001
520-774-0088
Toll-free 800-744-2008

Yogurt Parfait

"When we lived in Hinsdale, Illinois, a suburb of Chicago, we used to breakfast at the Egg Harbor Restaurant," said Innkeeper Sally Krueger. "Here's my version of their 'Shawna's Sunup.'" Makes 1 serving.

- ¼ cup low-fat granola (see Lower-Fat Granola recipe from the Weare-House, page 123)
- ¼ cup fresh berries or bite-size melon pieces
- ¼ cup nonfat vanilla yogurt
- 4 to 6 kiwi or strawberry slices, pressed against the glass
- ¼ banana, peeled and cut in bite-size pieces
- ¼ cup nonfat strawberry yogurt (or your favorite flavor)
- 2 to 3 slices Granny Smith apple
- 1 teaspoon raisins
- 1 teaspoon walnuts, chopped

- ■ Layer the granola, berries or melon, vanilla yogurt, kiwi or strawberry slices, banana, and strawberry yogurt in order into a parfait glass. Top with apple slices, and sprinkle with raisins and chopped nuts.
- ■ "Serve with a toasted English muffin, which has also been sprinkled with raisins and walnuts, a la Egg Harbor."

Wedgwood Inns

*W*hen Carl Glassman and Dinie Silnutzer-Glassman decided to make career changes, they did their research, worked in the hospitality industry, and then threw caution to the wind. A nineteenth-century home came up for sale, one that Carl had noticed for quite some time, and they started in on the major restoration needed.

The resulting Wedgwood House, named after their collection of china, opened in 1982, just a few blocks from the village center of this historic Bucks County river town. But that was just the beginning — it turned out they enjoyed innkeeping so much, they restored other inns, and now teach classes to aspiring innkeepers, as well.

Their bed-and-breakfasts are nineteenth-century homes on more than two acres of landscaped grounds. Guests can enjoy the gardens, gazebo, and a game of croquet, played in traditional costume, at tea-time in the summer. In the winter, tea and treats are enjoyed fireside in the parlor.

Dinie and Carl offer fresh-baked pastries, warm comforters, a glass of homemade almond liqueur before bed, and other touches to make guests comfortable. They host a number of special events, including historic reenactments, romantic getaways, relaxation retreats and other events created purely for guests' enjoyment.

Wedgwood Inns
111 West Bridge Street
New Hope, PA 18938
215-862-2520
Fax 215-862-2570

Apple Dutch Babies

Innkeeper Carl Glassman brought back this recipe from a Kibbutz in Israel, where he volunteered one summer. He picked apples from the Kibbutz orchards when making these classic "Dutch babies." In Israel, this was served with maple syrup to pour on top, but most guests at the Wedgwood find the fruit and nut mixture sweet enough. Makes 2 servings.

½ cup egg substitute (or 2 eggs, or 4 egg whites)
½ cup flour
½ cup skim milk
dash nutmeg
2 apples, peeled, cored, and chopped
dash sugar
dash cinnamon
¼ cup chopped walnuts
1 tablespoon raisins
2 pats canola margarine

- Preheat oven to 400 degrees.
- Mix egg, flour, milk, and nutmeg together with a whisk.
- Chop the apples and toss with cinnamon and sugar. Then add nuts and raisins to apples.
- Place 1 pat of margarine in each 9-ounce ramekin and place in oven for 5 minutes. Remove hot dishes from oven and ladle ½ cup of batter into each.
- Top with a generous scoop of the apple, nut, and raisin mixture. Bake 15 to 20 minutes or until puffed up and golden brown. Sprinkle with powdered sugar and serve immediately.

The Stout Trout Bed & Breakfast

*I*nnkeeper Kathleen Fredricks admits she doesn't cook low-fat by nature — being raised in Wisconsin dairy country, using tons of butter is only too easy. But she developed this pancake recipe for guests with dietary restrictions or those who just prefer a lower-fat meal.

Kathy found this former fishing lodge, located on Gull Lake in the Hayward Lakes region, when she returned to her home state after living in California. The building, complete with paint-on-velvet Elvis, needed a year's worth of major work. She gutted it and set to work, keeping only the original plank floors, and creating four large guestrooms.

Guests dine downstairs in the great room overlooking Gull Lake. In the winter, the forty acres behind the bed-and-breakfast are popular with cross-country skiing guests. In the summer, guests can fish for bass out front, or trout fish, canoe or tube the Namekagon River, ride horses, swim, or berry-pick nearby. The bed-and-breakfast's rowboat, canoes, and bikes are available for guests' use.

The Stout Trout
Bed & Breakfast
W4244 County Highway F
Springbrook, WI 54875
715-466-2790

Apple Oatmeal Pancakes

Innkeeper Kathleen Fredricks often makes these pancakes for winter guests who want extra energy for cross-country skiing on the 40 acres behind the bed-and-breakfast or in the famous Birkebeiner ski race in nearby Cable and Hayward, Wisconsin. Makes 16 pancakes.

          1 cup flour
          1 cup quick-cooking oats
        $\frac{1}{2}$ cup cornmeal
          4 teaspoons baking powder
        $\frac{1}{2}$ teaspoon baking soda
        $\frac{1}{2}$ teaspoon salt
        $\frac{1}{4}$ cup sugar
          2 eggs, separated
        $\frac{1}{4}$ (or less) oil
$2\frac{1}{4}$ to $2\frac{3}{4}$ cups buttermilk, depending on desired thickness
          1 tart apple, grated

- Mix flour, oats, cornmeal, baking powder, baking soda, salt, and sugar.
- Blend together egg yolks, oil, buttermilk, and grated apple. Mix dry and wet ingredients together.
- Beat egg whites until stiff, and then fold the whipped egg whites into the apple-flour mixture. Mix only until flour is dampened.
- Fry on a hot griddle.

Big Bay Point Lighthouse Bed & Breakfast

*A*ppetites are a little larger in this neck of the woods, thirty miles up the road from Marquette in Michigan's beautiful and wild Upper Peninsula. Hiking to waterfalls or through the woods, fishing, mountain biking, cross-country skiing, rock climbing, and canoeing are all offered near Big Bay, population 250. And it's all done in crisp, clean Lake Superior air.

This lighthouse, perched on a sixty-foot cliff over Lake Superior, went into operation in 1896. Two families lived here, one in each side of the duplex home. Ninety years later, it was a decommissioned lighthouse that was turned into a bed-and-breakfast.

The three innkeepers are former guests who came up from Chicago after reading about the lighthouse, its fifty acres of surrounding woods, and the view of the lake and the Huron Mountains from the lantern. Avid preservationists, they wanted the opportunity to live and work here, so they bought it and made some important changes. They enjoy meeting guests from the United States and other countries who have read about the chance to stay overnight in a lighthouse B&B.

Big Bay Point Lighthouse
Bed & Breakfast
3 Lighthouse Road
Big Bay, MI 49808
906-345-9957

Apple Pancakes

These pancakes have been requested frequently by guests, especially since a travel writer who stayed at the inn raved about them in the Minneapolis, Minnesota, newspaper. Innkeeper Linda Gamble serves them with homemade applesauce, which often takes the place of syrup. Makes 16 pancakes.

- 1 cup oatmeal flour (see below)
- 1 cup flour
- 1 cup whole-wheat flour
- 2 tablespoons sugar
- 1 tablespoon baking powder
- ¾ teaspoon salt
- 2¼ cup apple cider
- 3 eggs or ¾ cup egg substitute, thawed
- 2 tablespoons canola oil
- 2 large apples, peeled and grated

- ■ Preheat griddle to 400 degrees.
- ■ Make oatmeal flour by placing 1 cup uncooked old-fashioned rolled oats into a food processor, and process until oatmeal is the consistency of flour.
- ■ Combine oatmeal flour, flour, whole-wheat flour, sugar, baking powder, and salt, and mix well.
- ■ Add apple cider, eggs, oil, and apples and mix just until moistened.
- ■ Bake on griddle until top bubbles and edges are dry. Turn and bake on the other side until golden brown.

Applesauce

- 8 large apples, peeled, cored, and cut in quarters
- ½ cup water
- ¼ cup brown sugar
- 1 teaspoon cinnamon

- ■ Place apples and water in pan. Cover and bring to a boil. Simmer for 15 minutes. Add sugar and cinnamon; simmer 5 minutes. Place in a covered bowl and cool in refrigerator before serving.

The Queen Victoria®
Bed & Breakfast Country Inn

*O*ne of the Queen Victoria's most popular features is its central location in the historic district, where most of Cape May's attractions are within a few blocks of the inn. The Queen Victoria encompasses several buildings, and the beach and shops are within blocks — the inn even has a stable of bicycles for guests' use.

The nation's first seaside resort, Cape May offers guests the opportunity to enjoy a legacy of architectural and natural riches, including bird-watching at the well-known Cape May Point.

Travel writers from across the country have featured the Queen Victoria in a variety of magazines. The *Washington Post* chose the Queen Victoria as one of seven perfect places to escape those cold-weather blahs in "Wonderful Winter Inns." The Sherwin-Williams Company used the inn to illustrate its line of Victorian paints.

Innkeepers Dane and Joan Wells have made the inn a royal feast for all the senses with classical music, homemade quilts, ceiling fans to whisk the healthy ocean air, and of course a hearty breakfast in the morning and a proper tea in the afternoon.

The inn features a comfortable library, stocked with books and magazines about art, antiques, architecture, birding, and travel; two parlors, one with a fireplace and player piano for old-fashioned entertainment; and a wide selection of comfortable rooms and luxury suites.

The Queen Victoria
Bed & Breakfast Country Inn
102 Ocean Street
Cape May, NJ 08204
609-884-8702

Applesauce Bread Pudding

"As more of our guests are cutting down on their egg consumption, we have been looking for more main dishes which use fewer eggs," said Innkeeper Joan Wells. "This bread pudding is perfect — not too sweet, yet hearty enough for a good start to the morning." Makes 12 servings.

       nonstick cooking spray
16 slices cinnamon or raisin bread
2 cups applesauce
1 cup brown sugar
4 teaspoons cinnamon
½ teaspoon nutmeg
1 cup raisins, optional
3 cups skim milk
4 eggs
1 tablespoon vanilla

- Preheat oven to 350 degrees.
- Fit half of the bread on the bottom of a 3-quart glass baking dish which has been sprayed with nonstick cooking spray. Cut bread to fit as necessary. Spread applesauce on top.
- Mix brown sugar, cinnamon, and nutmeg, and sprinkle on top of applesauce, followed by raisins, if desired, and remaining bread.
- In a separate bowl, beat milk, eggs, and vanilla. Pour over ingredients in baking dish. (May be prepared in advance to this point and refrigerated, covered.)
- Bake at 350 degrees for 45 to 60 minutes until lightly puffed and browned.

The Inn at 410 Bed & Breakfast

"The place with the personal touch," the Inn at 410 offers four seasons of hospitality. A scrumptious gourmet breakfast is served in Innkeepers Howard and Sally Krueger's dining room each morning; the aroma of home-baked cookies greets guests at the end of their daily excursions.

Ideally located just blocks from historic downtown Flagstaff, the Inn at 410 can serve as a home base for a northern Arizona getaway. Many restaurants, cafes, shops, and galleries are within walking distance of the inn. Day trip destinations from the inn include Grand Canyon National Park, Sedona and Oak Creek Canyon, and the Painted Desert and Petrified Forest.

The inn has nine distinctive suites. Several have private entrances, fireplaces, or whirlpools. One suite is accessible to wheelchairs.

In the dining room, guests are served a full breakfast that features low-fat, low-cholesterol recipes. The inn's spacious parlor, trimmed with oak and furnished with antiques, is a relaxing place to sip hot cider and curl up with a book in front of the fireplace. The gazebo, surrounded by perennial gardens, offers summer guests an intimate retreat for afternoon iced tea.

The Inn at 410 Bed & Breakfast

410 North Leroux Street
Flagstaff, AZ 86001
520-774-0088
Toll-free 800-744-2008

Apricot-Almond Couscous

"We serve this unusual breakfast to our vegan guests," said Innkeeper Sally Krueger. Home cooks will enjoy it for other meals, as well. Makes 2 servings.

2 tablespoons slivered almonds, chopped
2 tablespoons shredded coconut
4 dried apricots
1 teaspoon honey, optional
2 tablespoons boiling water
¾ cup couscous
¾ cup boiling water
dash cinnamon
fresh fruit for garnish

- Preheat oven to 350 degrees.
- Spread almonds and coconut on a large flat baking sheet and toast in the oven until golden brown, about 10 minutes. Set aside to cool.
- Chop the apricots. Put them in a small bowl with honey and the 2 tablespoons boiling water. Let sit until apricots are softened, about 10 minutes.
- Five minutes before serving, measure couscous into a medium bowl. Add the ¾ cup boiling water, cover tightly with plastic wrap or a plate. Let stand 5 minutes.
- Stir to fluff couscous. Drain liquid from apricots and stir into couscous. If couscous is still a little hard, cover and let steam 1 to 2 minutes more. Divide prepared couscous among 2 plates or bowls. Sprinkle with a dash of cinnamon. Top each plate with half of the toasted nut-coconut mixture. Serve warm with a garnish of fresh fruit.

The Pentwater Inn

*B*uilt in 1868, the Pentwater Inn is ideal for exploring the beauty of Pentwater, Michigan. Mears State Park and quaint shops are within walking distance, or guests can borrow bikes at the inn and explore the sand dunes and countryside along the scenic Lake Michigan coast.

Innkeepers Donna and Quintus Renshaw purchased the Victorian house after returning from a six-year stay in England. Visitors can see the British influence in the decorating of the inn, which is furnished throughout with British and American antiques that they have collected over the years. The inn features six guestrooms, a hot tub, several porches, and a large parlor.

The Renshaws greet their guests with complimentary beverages and snacks each evening, and start each day with the aroma of homemade baked goods that accompany a memorable, full breakfast. Donna, who has a background in nutritional counseling and nursing, can provide special diets and low-fat breakfasts. Occasionally, weekends are designated with a special theme, such as "Chocolate Lover's Weekend," during which guests indulge in a variety of chocolate goodies, and low-fat entrées are always available upon request.

The Pentwater Inn

P.O. Box 98
180 East Lowell Street
Pentwater, MI 49449
616-869-5909

Baked Omelet Extraordinaire

The unbaked omelets can be frozen and thawed out the night before, or they can be kept overnight in the refrigerator and baked in the morning. "This is a lifesaver recipe for unexpected guests," noted Innkeeper Donna Renshaw. Makes 6 to 8 servings.

6 eggs, or equivalent egg substitute
2 teaspoons sugar
1 cup skim milk
4 ounces low-fat cream cheese (do not use nonfat)
1 16-ounce carton small-curd, low-fat cottage cheese
4 tablespoons oil
½ cup flour
1 teaspoon baking powder
1 cup low-fat ham, diced, optional
1 bunch of green onions, diced, optional
6 ounces canned mushrooms, optional
    canned or fresh jalapeño pepper, diced, "for a bit of zip," optional
    nonstick cooking spray

- Preheat oven to 350 degrees.
- Beat eggs or egg substitute, sugar, milk, and cream cheese in a large mixing bowl.
- Stir in cottage cheese, oil, flour, baking powder, and any of the extras such as the ham or green onions.
- Ladle into 6 or 8 individual dishes or a quiche pan sprayed with nonstick cooking spray.
- Bake in 350-degree oven for 20 minutes for the individual omelets, or 35 to 45 minutes for the larger one. The omelets are done when they are just golden around the edge and puffed in the center.

Blue Harbor House

*J*ody Schmoll and Dennis Hayden have made hospitality into an art form here, welcoming guests to beautiful rooms and common spaces and serving outstanding breakfasts and dinners.

These transplanted Californians began innkeeping in Camden, selected for its appeal to travelers, who may come by car, boat, or bike. Their Blue Harbor House is a restored 1810 New England Cape home, with guestrooms in the main inn or in carriage house suites. All rooms have handmade quilts and antiques and a homey feel.

Guests are often found in a rocker on the porch or helping themselves to snacks and beverages in the sun porch, where they can play board games and cards and enjoy some conversation. Jody and Dennis make themselves available to answer questions about Camden and help plan hiking, biking, boating, or shopping excursions. Bali (the inn's black lab), as well as any puppy that might be in training here as a future seeing-eye dog, can greet guests who request canine company.

Breakfasts and by-reservation-only dinners often feature regional specialties, such as baked Maine apples, blueberry pancakes with blueberry butter, or a traditional Maine lobster dinner complete with a Blue Harbor House apron. Jody and Dennis are known for creating popular dinner and event packages that bring guests back again and again.

Blue Harbor House

67 Elm Street
Camden, ME 04843
Toll-free 800-248-3196
Fax 207-236-6523

Blueberry-Stuffed French Toast

Even if you don't have wild Maine blueberries, this recipe is delicious with fresh or frozen commercially-grown berries. Innkeeper Dennis Hayden created this dish to showcase Maine berries and syrup while offering a low-fat breakfast option. Makes 4 servings.

      6 ounces nonfat cream cheese
      6 ounces nonfat yogurt
      2 ounces nonfat sour cream
      1 8-ounce package egg substitute
      1 cup skim milk
      1 teaspoon vanilla extract
    12 slices whole-wheat bread, crusts removed
      1 cup fresh Maine blueberries
    ½ cup frozen raspberries, crushed and drained
         powdered sugar for garnish
         Maine pure maple syrup

- In a bowl, mix cream cheese, yogurt, and sour cream to make the filling.
- In a separate bowl, mix egg substitute, milk, and vanilla to make the batter.
- Lightly coat 6 slices whole-wheat bread with filling, and place filling-side-up in a large pan. Sprinkle blueberries and raspberries generously on top of filling. Coat remaining 6 slices with filling and place filling-side-down on top of fruit, making a sandwich.
- Pour the batter over the bread and soak for 30 minutes.
- Cook on a griddle at medium heat until golden brown, turning several times.
- Slice diagonally, place on a large plate, and serve hot with powdered sugar and Maine maple syrup.

The Beazley House
Bed & Breakfast Inn

*J*im and Carol Beazley gave up careers — he was a photojournalist and she a registered nurse — to open Beazley House in 1981 as Napa's first bed-and-breakfast inn. "Some of our friends thought we were nuts," says Carol, "but the only thing we were afraid of was not getting the chance to try." The mansion they found is in old Napa, just a stroll from shopping and fine restaurants. Napa is only an hour north of San Francisco at the southern gateway of the world-famous Napa Valley wine country. It is a tree-shaded, river city surrounded by vineyards and wineries. Within minutes of the inn are wine touring, ballooning, cycling, hot mud baths, and mineral spas.

The Beazley House sits on half an acre of lawns and gardens. Visitors will see why it has been a Napa landmark since 1902 with its verdant lawns and bright flowers and welcoming stained glass front door. Elegant yet comfortable, the sitting room is to the left, and the beautiful gardens can be seen through the French doors straight ahead. The guestrooms are large and individually decorated with beautiful antiques and queen-sized beds. The Carriage House, nestled among gardens and tall trees behind the mansion, is the "country side" of the inn. In it, five charming, generous rooms with private spas and fireplaces await guests' discovery.

For breakfast, Beazley House serves a delicious buffet of fresh-baked muffins, crustless quiche, a variety of fresh fruits with yogurt, sweet orange juice, and a selection of teas and steaming coffee. Innkeepers Jim and Carol Beazley specialize in tasty, low-fat cuisine that pleases their guests.

The Beazley House
Bed & Breakfast Inn
1910 First Street
Napa, CA 94559
707-257-1649

Chili-Cheese Puff

Carol and Jim Beazley have made a concerted effort to specialize in low-fat cooking, converting favorite recipes and searching for new favorites. This recipe is a crowd-pleaser, and many guests don't even guess it's low in fat. Makes 8 servings.

       4 eggs
     1½ cups egg substitute
       ¼ cup plus 2 tablespoons flour
       1 teaspoon baking powder
       3 ounces nonfat cheddar cheese, grated
       3 ounces low-fat cheddar cheese, grated
     1½ cups 1 percent low-fat or nonfat cottage cheese
       1 4-ounce can green chili peppers, chopped
       ½ bunch scallions, chopped
          nonstick cooking spray

- Preheat oven to 325 degrees.
- In a blender, whirl together the eggs, egg substitute, flour, baking powder, cheddar cheeses, and cottage cheese. Pour into a large bowl. Add chili peppers and scallions.
- Spray 10-inch pie plate with nonstick cooking spray. Fill with mixture and bake in a 325-degree oven for 20 minutes.
- Reduce oven heat to 300 degrees until puff is set in the center (about 30 minutes). (This dish may be prepared the day before and kept in the refrigerator overnight, then baked the next morning.)

The Beazley House Bed & Breakfast Inn

*J*im and Carol Beazley gave up careers — he was a photojournalist and she a registered nurse — to open Beazley House in 1981 as Napa's first bed-and-breakfast inn. "Some of our friends thought we were nuts," says Carol, "but the only thing we were afraid of was not getting the chance to try." The mansion they found is in old Napa, just a stroll from shopping and fine restaurants. Napa is only an hour north of San Francisco at the southern gateway of the world-famous Napa Valley wine country. It is a tree-shaded, river city surrounded by vineyards and wineries. Within minutes of the inn are wine touring, ballooning, cycling, hot mud baths, and mineral spas.

The Beazley House sits on half an acre of lawns and gardens. Visitors will see why it has been a Napa landmark since 1902 with its verdant lawns and bright flowers and welcoming stained glass front door. Elegant yet comfortable, the sitting room is to the left, and the beautiful gardens can be seen through the French doors straight ahead. The guestrooms are large and individually decorated with beautiful antiques and queen-sized beds. The Carriage House, nestled among gardens and tall trees behind the mansion, is the "country side" of the inn. In it, five charming, generous rooms with private spas and fireplaces await guests' discovery.

For breakfast, Beazley House serves a delicious buffet of fresh-baked muffins, crustless quiche, a variety of fresh fruits with yogurt, sweet orange juice, and a selection of teas and steaming coffee. Innkeepers Jim and Carol Beazley specialize in tasty, low-fat cuisine that pleases their guests.

The Beazley House
Bed & Breakfast Inn
1910 First Street
Napa, CA 94559
707-257-1649

Creme Caramel Overnight French Toast

"When serving this treat, flip the pieces over onto the plate so the melted caramel sauce drips down all over your French toast. And since it already has its own syrup, you could top it with fresh fruit and a dollop of low-fat yogurt," says Innkeeper Carol Beazley. Makes 8 to 10 servings.

- $\frac{1}{4}$ cup low-fat margarine
- $\frac{1}{2}$ cup light corn syrup
- 1 cup brown sugar
- 1 loaf French bread
- $1\frac{1}{2}$ cups egg substitute
- $2\frac{1}{2}$ cups 1 percent milk
- $\frac{1}{3}$ cup sugar
- 1 tablespoon cinnamon
- 1 tablespoon vanilla extract
- $\frac{1}{2}$ tablespoon ground allspice

- Melt margarine and corn syrup together in a small saucepan. Stir in brown sugar and bring to a rolling boil. Let boil for 2 minutes.
- Remove from heat and stir down to a thick syrup. While the caramel is hot, pour into a baking pan (big enough for the slices of bread; see below) and chill in refrigerator for 10 to 20 minutes or until set. "You'll know it's ready when a light touch leaves your finger print on the caramel's surface."
- Slice the French bread into 8 to 10 thick slices, and arrange it in the pan over the caramel.
- Blend egg substitute and milk with sugar, cinnamon, vanilla, and allspice. Pour over bread. Cover and refrigerate overnight.
- In the morning, preheat oven to 350 degrees. Remove French toast from the refrigerator. Bake 45 minutes or until set in the middle. Flip each piece onto a plate to serve.

Yellow Rose — a Bed & Breakfast

*B*uilt in 1879 by the Charles Mueller family and restored in 1992–93 by former Innkeepers Jennifer and Cliff Tice, the Yellow Rose's interior and exterior reflect some of the finest craftsmanship available. Today, the Yellow Rose stands proudly among its contemporaries as a glowing example of splendor from the Victorian era. Situated in the quiet and elegant King William Historic District, the Yellow Rose has convenient access to downtown destinations by a trolley ride or a leisurely stroll along the famous San Antonio Riverwalk, only two blocks away.

In September 1996, J. Kit Walker and Deborah Field became the new owners, moving from New Mexico to enter the innkeeping profession. Deb, who spent twenty years in the restaurant business and then became a paralegal, and Kit, formerly an accountant, first looked for an inn in the Dallas area in order to be close to a niece and nephew. "We saw this place advertised in the Dallas paper, we came down here, and fell in love with it," Kit said. About six months later, they moved to San Antonio and took over innkeeping. Kit, an Albuquerque native, and Deb, originally from Council Bluffs, Iowa, enjoy recommending attractions and restaurants in their new home town. They also are proud to have opened a gallery on the main floor of the inn, featuring oil paintings and a few watercolors by New Mexican and Texan artists.

Yellow Rose —
a Bed & Breakfast
229 Madison
San Antonio, TX 78204
210-229-9903
Fax 210-229-1691

Fat-Free Omelet

"For variety, spoon picante sauce over cooked eggs or sprinkle with hot sauce. Instead of toast, serve with warmed corn tortillas," suggest Innkeepers J. Kit Walker and Deborah Field. Makes 2 servings.

> nonstick cooking spray
> ⅛ cup any variety onion, chopped
> ⅛ cup any variety bell pepper, sliced
> ⅛ cup celery, diced
> ⅛ cup any variety mushrooms
> 5 egg whites
> salt and pepper to taste

- Spray skillet with cooking spray, even if you are using a nonstick pan.
- Place celery, peppers, and onions in skillet and cook over moderate heat until onions are clear. Add mushrooms and heat only slightly. Do not allow mushrooms to give up their water. However, if they do start to give up liquid, spoon some of the liquid out of the pan before adding egg whites.
- In a small bowl, slightly beat the egg whites (5 to 6 good beats will do).
- Gently add the beaten whites to the sautéed vegetables in the skillet and cook over low heat. Use a fork to break small openings in the egg mixture and allow the egg white to cook. Do not stir as you might when cooking scrambled eggs. Turn omelet over once in skillet to thoroughly cook the egg mixture. Add salt and pepper to taste.

Pine Meadow Inn

*P*ine Meadow Inn is a large, country home built on a wooded knoll, and styled after a Midwestern farmhouse. Upstairs are four sunny bedrooms, always with fresh flowers and a feeling of comfortable warmth. Downstairs is the sitting room with a fireplace and library for guest use. The dining room has a large bay window that allows guests to bask in the morning sunshine, and the French doors open to the back yard herb and English cutting gardens. Also in the back yard are a grassy area for sunbathing, a large deck for relaxing, and a hot tub under the towering pines. Below the gardens is a lovely Koi pond and waterfall. The front of the house features a wrap-around porch with wicker chairs and rockers to relax in while enjoying morning coffee or evening tea.

The inn looks out on the four-acre meadow Innkeepers Nancy and Maloy Murdock call their front yard. Guests can enjoy a panoramic view of Mt. Walker and Mt. Sexton to the east and Buckhorn Mountain to the west. To the rear and sides of the inn are five acres of private forest, featuring walking paths and secluded sitting areas. The inn is located in Merlin, Oregon, the gateway to the scenic area of the Rogue River, near Grants Pass. Nearby are gourmet restaurants, golfing, wineries, and rafting, fishing, and swimming on the Rogue River.

Nancy and Maloy, who moved from the San Francisco area in 1991 to pursue their ten-year-long dream of building a B&B retreat, promise a delicious, healthy start to the day with fresh fruit (home-grown in season), home-baked breads and pastries, and other specialties of the house.

Pine Meadow Inn
1000 Crow Road
Merlin, OR 97532
Phone and fax 541-471-6277
Toll-free 800-554-0806

Fresh Veggie Frittata

"Our guests particularly enjoy this dish during the growing season, when they're able to stroll through our vegetable and fruit garden to see where the onions, asparagus, zucchini, and dill are grown!" said Innkeeper Nancy Murdock. Makes 10 servings.

½ cup asparagus tips
1 medium zucchini, sliced and quartered
1 cup fresh mushrooms, chopped
6 eggs
   egg substitute equal to 6 eggs
2 cups nonfat cottage cheese
2 cups low-fat mozzarella cheese, grated
½ cup green onions, chopped
1 teaspoon fresh dill, snipped
   nonstick cooking spray
   extra dill for garnish

- Preheat oven to 350 degrees.
- Lightly sauté asparagus tips, zucchini, and mushrooms. Be careful not to overcook.
- Combine eggs and egg substitute and beat until light and fluffy. Mix in cottage cheese and mozzarella cheese. Add green onions, sautéed vegetables, and dill, mixing until well blended.
- Pour into a 9 x 13-inch baking dish coated with nonstick cooking spray. Sprinkle top with more dill. Bake in a preheated oven at 350 degrees for 1 hour, or until knife inserted in the center comes out clean. To use individual ramekins, reduce baking time to 30 minutes.

The Inn at One Main Street

The Inn at One Main Street is a decorative shingled Victorian with Queen Anne accents, an open front porch, and a two-story turret. Surrounded by a white picket fence and landscaped grounds, the inn is an attractive introduction to the charming three-hundred-year-old village of Falmouth.

The inn was built in 1892 by the Swift family, well-known area merchants. In its first century, the house had several private owners before openings its doors in the 1950s as "The Victorian House," a guest house. The inn is ideally situated in the midst of the Historic District at the west end of Main Street, where the road to Woods Hole begins. Just off the Village Green, the inn is within walking distance to a bike path, beaches, tennis and racquetball, shops, restaurants, and galleries. Located within a short driving distance are Cape Cod National Seashore, whale watching, Provincetown, Plimouth Plantation, Boston, Woods Hole Marine Exhibits and Aquarium, and more.

Innkeepers Mari Zylinski and Karen Hart, friends since high school, provide a personal touch so that guests can escape the hustle and bustle of the real world. A full gourmet breakfast, served in the dining room, might feature tasty specialties such as gingerbread pancakes or Cape Cod cranberry pecan waffles. Breakfasts include chilled juices, fresh fruit, a variety of homemade scones or muffins, and freshly brewed coffee or tea.

The Inn at One Main Street

One Main Street
Falmouth, MA 02540
508-540-7469
Toll-free 888-AT-1-MAIN

Gingerbread Pancakes

"You may want to add more milk and reduce the molasses when doubling and tripling the recipe. It makes the pancakes a little lighter," suggest the innkeepers. Makes 4 to 6 pancakes.

- 1 cup flour
- 1½ teaspoons baking powder
- ½ teaspoon cinnamon
- ½ teaspoon ginger
- dash cloves
- ½ cup skim or 1 percent milk
- 3 tablespoons molasses
- 1 tablespoon vegetable oil
- 1 egg, slightly beaten

- Mix flour, baking powder, cinnamon, ginger, and cloves in a large bowl.
- In a separate bowl, stir milk, molasses, vegetable oil, and egg together. Combine milk mixture with dry ingredients.
- Cook on a preheated electric griddle at 350 degrees until golden brown on both sides.
- Serve with light whipped cream (instead of butter) and warm maple syrup.

Pine Meadow Inn

*P*ine Meadow Inn is a large, country home built on a wooded knoll, and styled after a Midwestern farmhouse. Upstairs are four sunny bedrooms, always with fresh flowers and a feeling of comfortable warmth. Downstairs is the sitting room with a fireplace and library for guest use. The dining room has a large bay window that allows guests to bask in the morning sunshine, and the French doors open to the back yard herb and English cutting gardens. Also in the back yard are a grassy area for sunbathing, a large deck for relaxing, and a hot tub under the towering pines. Below the gardens is a lovely Koi pond and waterfall. The front of the house features a wrap-around porch with wicker chairs and rockers to relax in while enjoying morning coffee or evening tea.

The inn looks out on the four-acre meadow Innkeepers Nancy and Maloy Murdock call their front yard. Guests can enjoy a panoramic view of Mt. Walker and Mt. Sexton to the east and Buckhorn Mountain to the west. To the rear and sides of the inn are five acres of private forest, featuring walking paths and secluded sitting areas. The inn is located in Merlin, Oregon, the gateway to the scenic area of the Rogue River, near Grants Pass. Nearby are gourmet restaurants, golfing, wineries, and rafting, fishing, and swimming on the Rogue River.

Nancy and Maloy, who moved from the San Francisco area in 1991 to pursue their ten-year-long dream of building a B&B retreat, promise a delicious, healthy start to the day with fresh fruit (home-grown in season), home-baked breads and pastries, and other specialties of the house.

Pine Meadow Inn

1000 Crow Road
Merlin, OR 97532
Phone and fax 541-471-6277
Toll-free 800-554-0806

Granny Smith Oatmeal Waffles

If you're in a hurry, you can make pancakes for this batter without the one-hour wait. For pancakes, reduce oil to 2 tablespoons. Makes 10 to 12 pancakes or 4 to 6 waffles.

1 ½ cups flour
1 cup old-fashioned rolled oats
2 teaspoons baking powder
1 ½ teaspoons cinnamon
1 teaspoon baking soda
½ teaspoon salt
½ teaspoon nutmeg
½ teaspoon vanilla extract
1 ½ cups nonfat buttermilk
2 tablespoons brown sugar or honey
1 egg
egg substitute equal to 2 eggs
4 tablespoons oil
2 medium Granny Smith apples, grated

- Mix flour, oats, baking powder, cinnamon, baking soda, salt, and nutmeg.
- Add vanilla, buttermilk, brown sugar or honey, egg, egg substitute, and oil. Mix all together by hand, using as few strokes as possible, then gently fold in the grated apple. The batter should be thick.
- Let batter sit for 1 hour before using.
- Bake in a preheated waffle iron until done. Especially good topped with home-made chunky applesauce, warmed in the winter, or fresh strawberries in the summer.

The Waverly Inn

*B*uilt in 1989, the Waverly Inn graces the town of Hendersonville, North Carolina. The town is a unique blend of cosmopolitan tastes and small town atmosphere. The restaurants are wonderful, and the shopping superb. Whether shoppers are looking for antiques, mountain crafts, unique clothing or gifts, downtown is within easy walking distance of the inn. The Biltmore Estate, Carl Sandburg Historic Site, Blue Ridge Parkway, and Chimney Rock/Lake Lure are just a few of the nearby destinations.

Recently renovated and listed in the National Register of Historic Places, the Waverly Inn is Hendersonville's oldest inn. Cited in national publications such as the *New York Times, Vogue,* and *Southern Living,* the Waverly offers personal service, breath-taking scenery year-around, and hospitality as it was meant to be. The inn boasts fourteen unique guestrooms, with a variety of beds and room designs.

The full breakfast always includes fresh fruit, stone ground grits, eggs, cereal, French toast or pancakes, homemade jams, preserves, fresh coffee, juice, and more. Guests comment on Innkeepers John and Diane Sheiry and Darla Olmstead's friendly hospitality, and the Waverly was named "One of the Top Ten Bed-and-Breakfasts in the USA" in 1993.

The Waverly Inn
783 North Main Street
Hendersonville, NC 28792
704-693-9193
Fax 704-692-1010

John's Buckwheat Pancakes

Innkeepers Diane and John Sheiry try to incorporate the use of whole grains into their diets as much as possible. This recipe is a favorite of both their family and their guests. Makes 16 pancakes.

   2 cups buckwheat flour
   2 cups buttermilk
   4 eggs, or equivalent egg substitute
   4 teaspoons baking powder
   1 teaspoon baking soda
  ½ teaspoon salt, optional
   2 tablespoons butter (or low-fat substitute)

- Mix buckwheat flour, buttermilk, eggs or egg substitute, baking powder, baking soda, salt, and low-fat butter substitute thoroughly.
- Let stand 15 minutes. Beat again.
- Spoon onto griddle or grill. Wait until tiny bubbles show up around the edges, then flip and cook until center bounces back when touched lightly.

Grant Corner Inn

*B*reakfast is such a special event at Santa Fe's Grant Corner Inn that it is open to the public by reservation. Innkeeper Louise Stewart has earned a great reputation for the inn's food, as well as the 12 guestrooms. How good is breakfast? So good that Louise's Grant Corner Inn cookbook is a best seller among guests who want to take a breakfast home with them!

Louise was born into an innkeeping family, and she's continued the tradition, raising her daughter, "Bumpy," at the inn. Louise's husband, Pat Walter, transformed a three-story Colonial home, right in downtown Santa Fe, into a romantic inn, complete with white picket fence and gazebo. It took nine long months of major renovation before the inn opened in 1982.

The home was built for the Winsor family, whose photo, among others of the home's residents over the years, hangs in the hallway. The dining rooms and parlor are on the first floor, with guestrooms on the second and third floors. The decor includes Louise's collection of antiques, Indian art, and bunnies (every type except the live kind), which have multiplied wildly and are everywhere, from tea pots and napkin rings to door stops.

Grant Corner Inn

122 Grant Avenue
Santa Fe, NM 87501
505-983-6678

Kewpie's Baked Eggs with Shrimp

Ethel Hulbert Renwick is a world-renowned author, lecturer, and nutritionist. "Kewpie," as Innkeeper Louise Stewart knows her, has always been a special part of her family. Louise featured this popular recipe in her own cookbook. For folks whose diets still include eggs, this is a delicious way to use eggs without frying or additional high-fat ingredients. Makes 6 servings.

  3 onions, finely chopped
  3 green peppers, seeded and chopped
  4 tablespoons olive oil
  3 medium tomatoes, peeled, seeded, and finely chopped
     salt to taste
     pepper to taste
     chili powder to taste
12 large eggs
  6 large shrimp, cooked and shelled

■ Preheat oven to 350 degrees.
■ Sauté onions and green peppers in olive oil for 1 minute. Add tomatoes; cook until softened. Season with salt, pepper, and chili powder.
■ Spoon a little sauce into the bottom of 6 individual baking dishes or ramekins. Slip 2 eggs from their shells into each dish. Place a shrimp in the center of each ramekin, then bake at 350 degrees for 10 minutes, or until eggs are set.
■ This recipe may also be made in 1 large baking dish, baking at least 25 minutes or until eggs are set.

Garden Grove Bed & Breakfast

*N*estled in the countryside of Union Pier, a charming resort community along the shore of Lake Michigan, in the heart of Michigan's beautiful Harbor Country, lies the quiet retreat of Garden Grove Bed-and-Breakfast, operated by Mary Ellen and Ric Postlewaite. Garden Grove is a vintage 1925 cottage home that has been renovated and decorated with vibrant colors and botanical influences to bring the garden indoors year-round. It has a comfortable cottage feel, blending old and new with a colorful, whimsical flair in the four guestrooms and the common areas. Mary Ellen calls Garden Grove their "baby," because they opened on Labor Day weekend in 1993, and the original renovation took nine months.

The inn features original wood floors throughout and beautiful garden views from all windows. There are decks and porches prepared for enjoying the gardens and warm days, as well as a sun-porch for less cooperative weather. The back garden features an outdoor hot tub for guest use and there are mountain bikes to borrow to tour the countryside. The dining room, parlor, and den feature a fireplace, games, video library, snacks, and reading materials. Breakfast is served on colorful china at individual dining tables.

Garden Grove Bed & Breakfast
9549 Union Pier Road
Union Pier, MI 49129
616-469-6346

Luscious Lemon Pancakes

"We serve these light, fluffy pancakes through the spring as the weather turns light and fresh as well," said Innkeeper Mary Ellen Postlewaite. The delicate tart lemon taste is nicely offset by the rich blueberry sauce, and the pancakes are a beautiful golden color. These pancakes are best if mixed immediately before cooking. Makes 8 medium pancakes.

1 cup flour
1 tablespoon sugar
1 teaspoon baking powder
½ teaspoon baking soda
½ teaspoon salt
  grated rind of 1 lemon
1 egg
2 tablespoons corn oil
1 8-ounce carton lemon yogurt
  juice of 1 lemon

- Mix flour, sugar, baking powder, baking soda, salt, and lemon rind. Add egg, oil, yogurt, and lemon juice. Batter will be slightly thick and puffy.
- Cook on a hot griddle. "They cook quickly," Mary Ellen warns.
- Serve with blueberry syrup or Blueberry Sauce.

Blueberry Sauce

1 cup blueberry jam
2 teaspoons grape juice

- Heat jam and juice in an uncovered, microwave-safe serving container about 2 minutes at high power, stirring once or twice during heating.
- Stir before serving.

Park Row Bed & Breakfast

*N*ot many inns draw guests just because of the innkeeper's collection of cookbooks or the fact that the cookie jar is always full for raiding. But in this case, the innkeeper is Ann Burckhardt, a popular food writer for the *Star Tribune* of the Twin Cities. She aims to make breakfasts memorable for her guests, who read her writing for years before she "retired" into full-time innkeeping in 1995. They love to read in her cookbook "library" and enjoy, perhaps, Maple Chocolate Chip Cookies.

Ann opened St. Peter's first bed-and-breakfast in 1990, several years before retirement, as a new challenge. She commuted the 66 miles to the Twin Cities from this peaceful Minnesota River Valley town, home of Gustavus Adolphus College.

Her gingerbread-trimmed B&B is a Carpenter Gothic home, circa 1870. It immediately captivated her during her search for a B&B. It needed minimal renovation to be turned into a four-guestroom inn, which she decorated with antiques, queen-sized beds, and down comforters.

Park Row Bed & Breakfast
525 West Park Row
St. Peter, MN 56082
507-931-2495

Minnesota Wild Rice Pancakes

"This recipe came into being when I had a family with two vegetarian sons at Park Row for Gustavus Adolphus College graduation," explained Innkeeper Ann Burckhardt. "For these strict vegetarians (no egg, no milk), I used rice milk from the local food co-op and skipped the egg. The crunchy texture of the pancakes makes them very satisfying." Makes 3 to 4 servings.

> 1 egg
> 1 cup flour
> ¾ cup milk, skim or 1 percent
> 1 tablespoon sugar
> 2 tablespoons vegetable oil, preferably canola
> 3 teaspoons baking powder
> ½ teaspoon salt
> 1 cup cooked wild rice
> ¾ cup pecans, finely chopped
>   real maple syrup
>   nonstick cooking spray

- In a 4-cup measuring cup, beat egg with rotary (hand) beater. Beat in flour, milk, sugar, oil, baking powder, and salt, mixing just until smooth.
- Heat pancake griddle (well-seasoned or nonstick) over medium-high heat. Remove from heat and spray griddle with nonstick spray.
- For each pancake, pour about 3 tablespoons batter from ¼-cup-size measuring cup. Typical griddle will hold 4 pancakes.
- Immediately sprinkle each cake with kernels of wild rice and some chopped pecans. "The hand (freshly washed, of course) works best for this. Don't try to save time by adding wild rice to the pancake batter. The rice will soak up the milk and lose its distinctive texture."
- As soon as the pancake surface is covered with tiny bubbles, use a long-handled spatula to carefully turn the pancakes.
- Take pancakes to the table right off the griddle. Have little pitchers of syrup on the table for guests to share.

The Lynchburg Mansion Inn
Bed & Breakfast

*T*he Lynchburg Mansion is a 9,000-square-foot Spanish Georgian Mansion situated on a half acre in the Garland Hill Historic District, which is on the National Register of Historic Places and is a designated Virginia Landmark. The inn was built in 1914 for James R. Gilliam, Sr., president of five coal companies, the Lynchburg Shoe Company, and six banks throughout the state.

Guests arrive driving under the columned porte-cochere. Twenty-two immense columns ring the 105-foot Spanish tiled veranda, the ideal location for a wedding or other special occasion. The double door entry opens onto a fifty-foot Grand Hall with soaring ceilings and unequaled cherry and oak woodwork, including great wide cherry columns and thick paneled cherry wainscoting. The oak and cherry main staircase winds up three stories and has 219 balustrades. The second floor is as extravagant as the first. The original central vacuum system, patented in 1907, remains.

The Lynchburg Mansion has become known for attention to detail and quality of service. All guestrooms are lavishly furnished and decorated with guests' comfort in mind. Bedchamber decor varies from the English-style Gilliam Room with mahogany four-poster, rice-carved king bed with steps, to the light and airy Country French Room done in crisp Laura Ashley and Battenburg lace.

Innkeepers Bob and Mauranna Sherman continue to indulge their guests in the morning with orange juice and freshly brewed coffee first, and a full, silver-service breakfast served in the formal dining room on gold-encrusted plates, fine china, crystal, and silver.

The Lynchburg Mansion Inn
Bed & Breakfast
405 Madison Street
Lynchburg, VA 24504
804-528-5400

Quick & Easy
Vegetarian Frittata

This fritatta is served at the Lynchburg Mansion Inn with jalapeño corn bread, salsa, and sliced potatoes, and garnished with parsley, herbs, and edible flowers. Makes 2 to 4 servings.

> egg substitute equal to 4 eggs
> ⅛ cup skim milk
> ¼ cup mixed variety low-fat cheese, shredded
> ⅓ cup tomato, diced
> ⅛ cup green bell pepper, diced
> ¼ cup cooked potatoes, diced
> ¼ cup whole-kernel corn
> 4 to 8 fine slices of mushroom
> nonstick cooking spray

- Preheat oven to 350 degrees.
- Spray an 8-inch pie pan with nonstick cooking spray.
- Beat egg substitute. Add milk, and beat again. Pour into pie pan.
- Sprinkle in cheese. With fork, press slightly so cheese does not sit on top. Sprinkle in tomatoes, peppers, potato, and corn. Place mushroom slices in each quarter, 1 or 2 per quarter.
- Bake at 350 degrees for about 25 minutes or until very light golden on top and set in center. "You can cook it at a higher temperature for a shorter time, and it puffs up a little more — just watch it," writes Mauranna Sherman.

Inn on the Rio

*B*uilt on an ancient site around buildings begun over two hundred years ago, the Inn on the Rio is a small, quaint, twelve-unit lodging in a quiet, residential setting. Nestled under centuries-old silver cottonwoods on the banks of the Rio Fernando, the Inn on the Rio is less than two miles from Taos Plaza and offers a relaxing atmosphere and easy access to Carson National Forest. Each room is decorated in a comfortable Southwestern style reflecting the rich and colorful heritage of northern New Mexico. Innkeepers Julie and Robert Cahalane provide a light, homemade breakfast in the inn's cozy gathering room, and a welcoming fire warms guests on cool mountain mornings.

The extraordinary lushness and beauty of Taos in the summer will entice visitors to take advantage of the inn's free all-terrain bicycles to explore the town of Taos. More challenging hiking and biking trails are just minutes away up Taos Canyon. Guests may choose to enjoy the inn's heated swimming pool, barbecue, and picnic facilities under the trees. Wagon rides and trail horses are available nearby.

The warm days and cold nights of the colorful autumn season invite a more leisurely appreciation of the diverse cultural and artistic events offered at this time of the year. The inn's location is convenient for all types of winter sports enthusiasts, as well. Cross country trails, family skiing, snow boarding, and ice skating facilities are nearby, as is Taos Ski Valley. The inn's proximity to town provides a wide variety of choices for shopping, dining, sight-seeing, and entertainment.

Inn on the Rio

Box 6529-NDCBU
910 East Kit Carson Road
Taos, NM 87571
505-758-7199
Toll-free 800-859-6752

Southwest Bake

The busy innkeepers at the Inn on the Rio especially enjoy this flavorful dish's make-ahead preparation. Guests enjoy a Southwest-style dish without excess calories or cholesterol. Makes 10 servings.

> nonstick cooking spray
> 1/2 pound low-fat turkey sausage
> 6 slices nonfat bread
> egg substitute equal to 6 eggs
> 1 cup skim or 1 percent milk
> 1 cup salsa
> 6 ounces sliced nonfat jalapeño cheese
> 6 ounces low-fat or nonfat cheddar cheese

- Brown sausage (don't add any oil). Crumble cooked sausage on a paper towel to absorb any excess oil.
- Lightly spray an 8 x 11-inch baking dish with nonstick cooking spray. Line the baking dish with the bread slices. Sprinkle the sausage over the bread.
- Mix the eggs, milk, and salsa together. Pour over the bread slices. Top with the jalapeño cheese slices. Cover with foil and refrigerate over night.
- At brunch or breakfast time, put casserole in a preheated 350-degree oven for 30 minutes.
- Take off foil and then add cheddar cheese and bake for 15 minutes more.
- Remove from oven and let cool 10 minutes before serving. Serve with extra salsa, hot or mild, and enjoy!

The Pentwater Inn

*B*uilt in 1868, the Pentwater Inn is ideal for exploring the beauty of Pentwater, Michigan. Mears State Park and quaint shops are within walking distance, or guests can borrow bikes at the inn and explore the sand dunes and countryside along the scenic Lake Michigan coast.

Innkeepers Donna and Quintus Renshaw purchased the Victorian house after returning from a six-year stay in England. Visitors can see the British influence in the decorating of the inn, which is furnished throughout with British and American antiques that they have collected over the years. The inn features six guestrooms, a hot tub, several porches, and a large parlor.

The Renshaws greet their guests with complimentary beverages and snacks each evening, and start each day with the aroma of homemade baked goods that accompany a memorable, full breakfast. Donna, who has a background in nutritional counseling and nursing, can provide special diets and low-fat breakfasts. Occasionally, weekends are designated with a special theme, such as "Chocolate Lover's Weekend," during which guests indulge in a variety of chocolate goodies, and low-fat entrées are always available upon request.

The Pentwater Inn

P.O. Box 98
180 East Lowell Street
Pentwater, MI 49449
616-869-5909

Tart Cherry Crepes

Scenic northwestern Michigan, with temperatures moderated by Lake Michigan, is prime cherry country. Innkeeper Donna Renshaw, a nutritional counselor, loves to serve healthy and delicious creations using this wonderful fresh fruit! Makes 6 servings.

1 cup flour
1 tablespoon sugar
4 eggs, or equivalent egg substitute
1½ cups milk
2 tablespoons oil (can be reduced to 2 teaspoons)

- Put flour, sugar, eggs or egg substitute, milk, and oil in a blender and blend until smooth.
- Lightly oil an 8-inch frying pan over medium-high heat. Pour about 2 tablespoons of batter in a pan and swirl to coat bottom of pan. When the top of the crepe is dry, flip and cook the other side for 45 seconds. Crepes should be very thin.
- Keep crepes warm in oven, and cover with a plate.

Tart Cherry Sauce

Blueberries or raspberries may be substituted for the cherries. For a gourmet touch, add 2 tablespoons of cherry liqueur to the sauce before serving.

2 cups frozen or fresh tart, pitted cherries
½ cup sugar
1 tablespoon cornstarch
powdered sugar for garnish

- Combine cherries, sugar, and cornstarch in a large saucepan. Cook over medium-high heat, stirring until sugar dissolves and sauce thickens.
- Fold crepes in half and in half again to form triangles. Place 2 on a plate and ladle sauce in the center.
- Dust with powdered sugar around the edges and serve.

Mast Farm Inn

*L*ocated a short distance from the Blue Ridge Parkway in the scenic town of Valle Crucis, the Mast Farm Inn, built in 1885, was first operated as an inn in the early 1900s by Finley Mast and his wife Josephine. In 1972, the Mast Farm was placed in the National Register of Historic Places as one of the best examples of a self-contained mountain homestead in the North Carolina high country.

The 18-room house and several out-buildings have been restored by the current owners, Francis and Sibyl Pressly. Originally a 13-bedroom, one-bath house, the main house now has nine large guestrooms. In addition, there are accommodations in three comfortably-furnished out-buildings: the Loom House, Blacksmith Shop, and Woodwork Shop. Rooms have simple, turn-of-the-century antiques and are tastefully decorated in the vintage of the early 1900s. Visitors will feel as though they are stepping back in time, without a loss of modern convenience.

Inn guests are treated to a hearty breakfast; something different is offered each day, but there are always homemade breads, jams, and fresh fruit. A family-style dinner is served to inn guests and others on weekday evenings and Sunday noon.

In the early 1900s, the hospitality of Finley and Josephine Mast added a personal touch to make their guests' stay memorable. Today, ninety years later, guests receive the same gracious attention from the Presslys and their staff.

Mast Farm Inn
P.O. Box 704
Valle Crucis, NC 28691
704-963-5857
Fax 704-963-6404

Three-Grain Pancakes

"Surprisingly light for pancakes made with whole grains, these scored high with the guinea pigs who helped test the recipes," said Sibyl Pressly, innkeeper. "Friends are thinking twice when I invite them to dinner these days."

With a few minor changes (see the egg alternatives), these pancakes are the perfect breakfast for the health-conscious guest. This batter holds up well ("It's good for late-comers!") and is better mixed at least 15 minutes before using. Makes 32 pancakes.

> 3 cups buttermilk
> 2 eggs (or 4 egg whites, or egg substitute equal to 2 eggs)
> ⅔ cup corn oil
> ½ cup yellow cornmeal
> ½ cup flour
> 1 cup whole-wheat flour
> 1 cup old-fashioned rolled oats
> 2 tablespoons baking powder
> ½ teaspoon baking soda
> ½ teaspoon salt
> 2 teaspoons sugar, optional
> nonstick cooking spray

- Beat buttermilk, eggs, and oil together in a large bowl.
- Mix remaining ingredients (cornmeal, flours, oats, baking powder, baking soda, salt, and sugar) together. Stir to mix well, then add to liquid mixture. Stir just enough to blend.
- Spray hot griddle with vegetable nonstick spray and drop pancake batter by the tablespoon onto griddle. Turn once only, when top of pancake is covered with bubbles. Remove to warm place when brown on the bottom and serve immediately with maple syrup, a fruit syrup, or applesauce.

The Ant Street Inn

*I*n historic Brehnam, Texas, home to bluebonnets and Blue Bell Ice Cream, the Ant Street Inn combines Deep South hospitality, warmth, and elegance with the conveniences and personal service of a first-class hotel. Centrally located, the inn is an inviting destination for an overnight or weekend stay while traveling for business or pleasure.

The fourteen guestrooms have been painstakingly restored to retain their original flavor while offering modern comfort and convenience. All have 12-foot ceilings, polished hardwood floors with Oriental rugs, stained glass, and more. The owners, Tommy and Pam Traylor, have furnished the inn with their collection of American antiques.

Breakfast includes chilled juices, fruit of the season, egg casseroles, fresh muffins, pastries, or other favorites discovered by Pam while she was working with *Southern Living* magazine's cooking school.

While in Washington County, guests can tour Blue Bell Creameries, the Antique Rose Emporium, the Brenham Heritage Museum, and the Star of the Republic Museum at Washington-on-the-Brazos State Park, among other sites. Shops and restaurants are just a short stroll from the inn's front door.

The Ant Street Inn
107 West Commerce
Brenham, TX 77833
409-836-7393
Fax 409-836-7595

Tejas Breakfast Cups

With 14 guestrooms at the Ant Street Inn, Innkeeper Pam Traylor makes this recipe in sufficient quantity to serve all her guests. Some type of egg dish is usually on the breakfast table, and, despite its low-fat nature, this is one of the most popular. Makes 4 servings.

     4 corn tortillas (approximately 6-inch)
        nonstick cooking spray
     1 12-ounce carton frozen egg substitute, thawed
     ½ teaspoon garlic salt
     ¼ teaspoon cumin
     1 tablespoon fresh cilantro or parsley, minced
     ¼ cup salsa
     1 tablespoon plus 1 teaspoon shredded Mexican cheese

- Preheat oven to 375 degrees.
- Cutting from the edge of a tortilla toward its center, make a 2-inch cut. Repeat for a total of 4 evenly spaced cuts. Spray each side of the tortilla with nonstick cooking spray and gently press into a muffin tin. Overlap edges of tortilla to form a cup. Bake at 375 degrees for about 5 minutes; keep warm.
- Combine egg substitute, garlic salt, and cumin in a heated skillet that was sprayed with cooking spray and cook, stirring occasionally. Add cilantro or parsley and cook until mixture is set.
- Spoon into prepared tortilla cups. Top each with salsa and cheese. Bake until cheese is melted.

Salisbury House

*W*ashington apples are just one of the fresh fruits that end up as breakfast fare at the Salisbury House. Innkeeper Cathryn Wiese and her mother, Mary, often pick berries at the region's berry farms or enjoy pears and apples from their own trees, and the fruit may end up in muffins, preserves, or on a fruit plate.

Breakfast is served in the dining room of this large, airy home. Downstairs, the home has refinished maple floors and beam ceilings. Upstairs are four guestrooms, all uniquely decorated, and a sun porch. Guests are welcome to play chess in the library, rock on the wrap-around porch, or enjoy the fireplace in the living room.

Mary, who was raised in Seattle, and Cathryn, who has been in Seattle for the past 15 years, opened their bed-and-breakfast in 1984, after living in San Diego for 18 years. Salisbury House is in the beautiful Capitol Hill neighborhood, walking distance to art museums, Volunteer Park, and shops and restaurants. Guests often leave their cars and hop a bus a block away to get to the University of Washington or to explore downtown Seattle's Pike Place Market, piers and Aquarium, historic district, and other attractions.

Salisbury House

750 16th Avenue East
Seattle, WA 98112
206-328-8682
Fax 206-720-1019

Apple Coffeecake

Because Washington apples are available nearly all year-round, guests at Salisbury House can enjoy the aroma of this coffeecake baking almost any morning. Innkeeper Cathryn Wiese allows some indulgence, using eggs and oil and sometimes nuts in this recipe. Makes 10 to 12 servings.

2 cups flour
1 teaspoon baking soda
2 eggs
½ cup vegetable oil
1 cup sugar
1 cup brown sugar
2 teaspoons cinnamon
½ teaspoon nutmeg
4 cups apples, peeled or unpeeled, cored, and diced
1 cup nuts, chopped, optional
  nonstick cooking spray

Topping
½ cup nuts, chopped, optional
⅓ cup sugar
⅓ cup brown sugar
1 teaspoon cinnamon

- Preheat oven to 350 degrees.
- Mix flour and baking soda in medium bowl.
- In a separate bowl, beat eggs slightly. Add oil, sugars, and spices. Mix in apples and nuts. Combine flour mixture with egg mixture. Batter will be thick and dry.
- To make topping, mix chopped nuts, sugars, and cinnamon.
- Spray 2 8-inch cake pans with nonstick spray, spread batter into pans, and sprinkle topping over both. Bake 45 minutes. Cool just enough to slice without crumbling, about 10 minutes.

The McCallum House

A low-fat, low-cholesterol breakfast is served family-style in the dining room of Nancy and Roger Danley, who have operated this home as a bed-and-breakfast since 1983, one of the first B&Bs to open in Texas.

The Danleys bought this 1907 home from the heirs of Jane and A. N. McCallum. A. N. was Austin's school superintendent for 39 years. Jane was a suffragist who helped organize the "Petticoat Lobby" for human service reforms in Texas (signs and other memorabilia grace the stairway). She served under two governors as secretary of state. They also raised five children in this large house, which Jane designed while she was pregnant with her fifth child.

Nancy and Roger started innkeeping as an experiment, with just one guestroom in 1983. Today, the Danleys have three guestrooms on the second floor, a garden apartment, and a large suite in the dormered third floor called "Jane's Loft," which Roger built.

Their inn is a popular destination for those visiting the University of Texas at Austin, about eight blocks away, or Austin's many attractions. The Danleys love Austin, a wonderful city close to the Texas Hill Country, and they're happy to help guests explore the area.

The McCallum House

613 West 32nd
Austin, TX 78705
512-451-6744
Fax 512-451-4752

Blueberry Gingerbread with Lemon Curd

Serve the lemon curd warm for the blueberry gingerbread, but it's also great cold. Makes 6 servings.

  1½ cups flour
  ½ cup "flour combo" (2 parts old-fashioned rolled oats and 1 part wheat bran, ground to a coarse flour in food processor)
  1 teaspoon cardamom
  1 teaspoon ginger
  1½ teaspoons baking soda
  2 egg whites, lightly beaten
  1 scant cup sugar
  ½ cup unsweetened applesauce
  1 cup nonfat yogurt or sour milk
  3 tablespoons molasses
    some grated orange rind — about half an orange
  1 cup blueberries (frozen are fine; knock off any ice crystals in a colander)
  3 tablespoons sugar (or coarsely chopped crystallized ginger)

Lemon Curd
  4 egg whites
  1 cup sugar
    juice and chopped rind of 2 lemons (or limes)

- Preheat oven to 350 degrees.
- In a large bowl, sift together "flour combo," cardamom, ginger, and baking soda.
- In a separate bowl, thoroughly combine beaten egg whites, sugar, applesauce, yogurt or sour milk, molasses, and chopped orange rind. Add liquid ingredients to dry and combine until just mixed.
- Put into "the largest pie plate you have" and sprinkle with the blueberries and sugar or crystallized ginger. Bake in a 350-degree oven for 20 to 30 minutes. Serve with lemon curd.
- To make the lemon curd: Beat egg whites lightly. Add sugar, lemon juice, and lemon rind. Mix well. Cook at medium power until thickened in a microwave about 4 minutes, but be sure to stir well every 45 seconds to 1 minute.

The Owl and the Pussycat
Bed & Breakfast

The Owl and the Pussycat Bed-and-Breakfast is a Queen Anne Victorian home built in the 1890s, furnished with antiques. The inn is perfectly located for guests with an interest in area sites. Many of historic Petersburg's attractions are just a brief stroll down High Street. Old Towne is close by, with restaurants within walking distance. High Street itself boasts attractive examples of various architectural styles, such as a Tidewater Colonial (1757), a classic Georgian (1762), Second Empire, as well as Greek Revival and Federal. Other nearby attractions include Petersburg National Battlefield, Pocahontas State Park, and the James River Plantations.

The inn features five guestrooms, all large and each one different from the other. Guests in the Owl Room can enjoy the turret overlooking the garden, while those in the Pussycat Room can relax on the private balcony. The Ribbon Plate room showcases a collection of ribbon plates mostly from Germany and England, the Sonnet Room houses a valued collection of poetry, and the Boat Room reflects a love of the water. In addition, Innkeepers Juliette, who grew up in Bath, England, and John Swenson have a spacious garden for guests to enjoy.

A full breakfast is served in the dining room and includes freshly made fruit breads or scones, and homemade jams and jellies. For a special occasion, guests can be served breakfast in their rooms.

The Owl and the Pussycat
Bed & Breakfast
405 High Street
Petersburg, VA 23803
804-733-0505
Fax 804-862-0694

Fruited Bran Bread

Innkeeper Juliette Swanson stresses low-fat, low-sugar, and high-fiber cooking and baking at her Owl and the Pussycat Bed-and-Breakfast. This bread has a wonderful aroma while baking, she notes, plus tastes great. Makes 1 loaf.

  1¾ cups unbleached flour
  ⅔ cup bran
  ¾ cup granulated cane juice or sugar
  2 tablespoons aluminum-free baking powder
  1 teaspoon baking soda
  3 teaspoons cinnamon
  1 teaspoon nutmeg
  ½ teaspoon allspice
  ¼ salt
  ¾ cup currants, or dates or dried apricots, chopped
  ¾ cup unsweetened applesauce
  1 cup low-fat buttermilk
  1 tablespoon lemon juice
    nonstick cooking spray

- Preheat oven to 350 degrees.
- Mix flour, bran, sugar, baking powder, baking soda, cinnamon, nutmeg, allspice, salt, and dried fruit together.
- Mix together applesauce, buttermilk, and lemon juice. Add to dry ingredients.
- Spread batter into a 9 x 5-inch bread loaf pan that has been sprayed with cooking spray.
- Bake for 60 minutes or until a toothpick inserted in the center comes out clean.

The Governor's Inn

*T*he Governor's Inn in Ludlow was built in 1890 by Vermont Governor William Wallace Stickney as a wedding present for his bride, Elizabeth Lincoln. Innkeepers Deedy and Charlie Marble have made sure the inn has retained the intimate feeling of a comfortable and elegant country house by furnishing the inn with family antiques, Oriental rugs, brass beds — and by warmly welcoming their guests.

Today, the inn welcomes overnight guests to the eight guestrooms, as well as diners who wish to enjoy Deedy's unique six-course dinners that emphasize local ingredients such as pumpkin, blueberries, New England seafood, and cranberries. Charlie specializes as the breakfast chef.

Deedy and Charlie, married for more than 33 years, left other successful careers — Charlie in construction, and Deedy as an artist and an executive director with the American Dental Association — to enter their lifelong dream of innkeeping. They opened this historic home, across from the village green, in 1982, and have since won numerous awards for cuisine and hospitality (they'll even pack a gourmet picnic lunch basket). The inn is located just one mile from Okemo Mountain ski area, for which Ludlow is well-known.

The Governor's Inn

86 Main Street
Ludlow, VT 05149
802-228-8830

Grandmother's Graham Bread

Yankee *magazine conducted a national recipe contest in 1987, and this recipe from the Governor's Inn "heirloom files" was a winner. "We recommend that you double the recipe, as it has a way of disappearing right before your eyes," suggests Innkeeper Deedy Marble. Makes 2 loaves.*

1 ⅞ cups milk
    2 tablespoons cider vinegar
1 ½ cups graham flour
    2 cups flour
    ½ cup brown sugar
    ½ cup molasses
    2 teaspoons baking soda
    1 teaspoon salt
        nonstick cooking spray

- Preheat oven to 350 degrees.
- Combine the milk and cider vinegar to make sour milk.
- Mix graham flour, flour, brown sugar, molasses, sour milk, baking soda, and salt together with an electric mixer.
- Pour into 2 greased 9 x 5-inch bread loaf pans. Bake for 30 minutes. Cool before slicing.

The Beazley House
Bed & Breakfast Inn

*J*im and Carol Beazley gave up careers — he was a photojournalist and she a registered nurse — to open Beazley House in 1981 as Napa's first bed-and-breakfast inn. "Some of our friends thought we were nuts," says Carol, "but the only thing we were afraid of was not getting the chance to try." The mansion they found is in old Napa, just a stroll from shopping and fine restaurants. Napa is only an hour north of San Francisco at the southern gateway of the world-famous Napa Valley wine country. It is a tree-shaded, river city surrounded by vineyards and wineries. Within minutes of the inn are wine touring, ballooning, cycling, hot mud baths, and mineral spas.

The Beazley House sits on half an acre of lawns and gardens. Visitors will see why it has been a Napa landmark since 1902 with its verdant lawns and bright flowers and welcoming stained glass front door. Elegant yet comfortable, the sitting room is to the left, and the beautiful gardens can be seen through the French doors straight ahead. The guestrooms are large and individually decorated with beautiful antiques and queen-sized beds. The Carriage House, nestled among gardens and tall trees behind the mansion, is the "country side" of the inn. In it, five charming, generous rooms with private spas and fireplaces await guests' discovery.

For breakfast, Beazley House serves a delicious buffet of fresh-baked muffins, crustless quiche, a variety of fresh fruits with yogurt, sweet orange juice, and a selection of teas and steaming coffee. Innkeepers Jim and Carol Beazley specialize in tasty, low-fat cuisine that pleases their guests.

The Beazley House
Bed & Breakfast Inn

1910 First Street
Napa, CA 94559
707-257-1649

Pineapple Bread

This sweet tea bread can be enjoyed all day long. Innkeeper Carol Beazley carefully adapted higher-fat recipes to get them to have the nutritional and lower-fat content she desired. Makes 36 servings: 3 small Bundt pans; 1 large Bundt and 1 small Bundt pan; or 3 bread loaf pans.

        2 tablespoons canola oil
        2 cups sugar
        3 eggs
        3 teaspoons vanilla extract
        1 20-ounce can crushed pineapple, drained
        1 cup unsweetened applesauce
    2 ½ cups unbleached flour
        3 teaspoons baking soda
        1 teaspoon baking powder
        1 cup low-fat buttermilk
        1 tablespoon cinnamon
        2 cups unbleached flour
           nonstick cooking spray

- Preheat oven to 325 degrees.
- In a large bowl, combine canola oil, sugar, eggs, vanilla, crushed pineapple, and applesauce.
- Then add the first 2 ½ cups of flour, baking soda, and baking powder, mixing until smooth. Stir in buttermilk, cinnamon, and additional 2 cups of unbleached flour.
- Spray pans with nonstick cooking spray. Fill each ⅔ full of batter and bake in a 325-degree oven for 45 minutes or until a toothpick comes out clean.

Clauser's Bed & Breakfast

*L*ocated 35 miles north of Orlando, where the gently rolling terrain of West Volusia County begins, Clauser's Bed-and-Breakfast sits in secluded country charm in Lake Helen, "The Gem of Florida." On the National Register of Historic Places, the property served as a lodging establishment at the turn of the century. Surrounded by many varieties of trees, the quiet aura sets Clauser's a world apart from today's fast pace.

Today, the bed-and-breakfast includes the original house, circa 1895, as well as a carriage house built by Innkeepers Tom and Marge Clauser in 1994. Designed to blend with the historic main house, the carriage house features relaxing porches and a tin roof. Some of the six rooms in the carriage house, as well as the two rooms in the original house, have whirlpool baths or soaking tubs, and most rooms have private, screened porches. Guests can enjoy an early morning cup of coffee on the porch or in the courtyard gardens as the sun peeks through the forest to the east. A full country breakfast follows.

The choices of activities around Clauser's are many and varied. Lake Helen has a historic district with turn-of-the-century homes, churches, and antique shops. DeLand, only seven miles away, has an old-fashioned downtown area with antique and gift shops, art galleries, museums, restaurants, and Stetson University. Cassadaga, a village world-renowned as a center for psychics and mediums, is nearby. Fun in the sun is only minutes away at New Smyrna Beach, Daytona Beach, several state parks, and a national wildlife preservation area. And of course the Orlando theme parks are about an hour away.

Clauser's Bed & Breakfast

201 East Kicklighter Road
Lake Helen, FL 32744
904-228-0310
Fax 904-228-2337

Applesauce Oatmeal Muffins

Should there be leftovers, "freeze 'em!" Innkeeper Marge Clauser recommends. Wrap baked muffins securely, and use within 30 days. These muffins reheat well in a micro-wave. Makes 12 muffins.

1½ cups oats (quick-cooking or old fashioned)
1¼ cups flour
¾ teaspoon cinnamon
1 teaspoon baking powder
¾ teaspoon baking soda
1 cup unsweetened applesauce
½ cup milk, skim or 1 percent
½ cup brown sugar, firmly packed
3 tablespoons vegetable oil
1 egg, or equivalent egg substitute

Topping 1
¼ cup quick-cooking oats
1 tablespoon firmly packed brown sugar
½ tablespoon margarine, melted

Topping 2
½ teaspoon cinnamon
2 tablespoons sugar

- Preheat oven to 400 degrees.
- Line muffin pan with paper liners.
- Combine oats, flour, cinnamon, baking powder, and baking soda.
- Add applesauce, milk, brown sugar, oil, and egg. Mix just until dry ingredients are moistened.
- Fill muffin cups almost full. Top muffin batter with either topping 1 or topping 2. For either topping, combine ingredients; sprinkle evenly over batter.
- Bake 20 to 22 minutes or until deep golden brown. Serve warm.

Desoto at Prior's Bed & Breakfast

*I*nnkeeper Mary Prior is used to cooking breakfast for large numbers of diners, and looks for easy recipes. "We had six members in our family, and all of our relatives lived out-of-state, so we often had guests for breakfast," said Mary.

Husband Richard, a building contractor who designed the house, and Mary discovered bed-and-breakfasts while overseas. "We have been to Europe seven times and just loved the B&Bs there, and we always said that was something we wanted to do," she said. They tried one room when the Summer Olympics try-outs came to town and liked it, as they expected.

Their contemporary home was built in 1991 in a quiet residential neighborhood about five minutes northeast of downtown St. Paul. The living room's twenty-foot vaulted ceiling overlooks the fireplace. Tall windows are perfect for viewing sunsets. The sundeck is perfect for bird-watching, in which the Priors have recently become interested. Guests have use of the refrigerator and microwave.

Desoto at Prior's

1522 Desoto Street
St. Paul, MN 55101
612-774-2695

Blueberry Muffins

"We have been making these muffins at our house for 40 years (since we were married) and we have never had a failure!" said Innkeeper Mary Prior. "We freeze our own blueberries and use them when the fresh season is over. They are very easy to freeze — just wash, drain, spread out on a cookie sheet, and freeze. When frozen, remove with a spatula to freezer bags. This way, they do not stick together and can be used as needed without defrosting a whole container." Makes 12 muffins.

　1　egg, beaten
　1　cup skim milk
　4　tablespoons margarine, softened or melted
　2　cups unbleached flour
　4　tablespoons sugar
　2　teaspoons baking powder
　⅔　teaspoon salt
　1　cup fresh or frozen blueberries

- Preheat oven to 425 degrees.
- Lightly grease muffin cups.
- Beat egg in a medium bowl, and add milk and margarine.
- Measure flour, sugar, baking powder, and salt, into flour sifter and sift directly into milk mixture. "It's very important not to overbeat the batter. Stir until just moistened."
- Add blueberries and stir until just blended. Spoon into greased muffin pans.
- Bake at 425 degrees for 15 to 20 minutes, or until a toothpick inserted in a muffin comes out clean.

Thimbleberry Inn Bed & Breakfast

*T*his new contemporary home, opened as a bed-and-breakfast in May 1993, features 375 feet of Lake Superior frontage and has a spectacular view of five of the Apostle Islands. The three guestrooms each have a private entrance and a working fireplace. Guests enjoy freshly brewed gourmet coffee and homemade muffins delivered to their rooms in Longaberger baskets a half hour prior to a full gourmet breakfast. Breakfast is served on the spacious deck, weather permitting, or in the dining area overlooking the islands. Innkeeper Sharon Locey loves cooking. She has entered and won several prizes in dairy bake-offs, has taught 4H food classes and a holiday foods class for two colleges, and is a field editor for a popular cooking magazine.

Thimbleberry Inn is located just south of Schooner Bay on Lake Superior. Its lovely wooded setting offers guests a quiet secluded getaway in which to walk among the trees on the forty-acre property or along the lake, or just relax in an outdoor Adirondack love seat and enjoy the restful sound of the waves lapping against the shore. Guests may be fortunate enough to see one of several eagles that soar along the lake shore. For the more adventuresome, the inn recently acquired a sailboat, and offer half-day and full-day trips among the Apostles. Bayfield is home to the Apostle Islands National Lakeshore.

Thimbleberry Inn
Bed & Breakfast
15021 Pageant Road
P.O. Box 1007
Bayfield, WI 54814
715-779-5757

Craisin Yogurt Muffins

"These muffins have been a favorite of our guests since we opened in 1993," said Sharon Locey. "They are very easy to prepare and the batter keeps well in the refrigerator for several days if you want to double the recipe. The yogurt makes for a very moist muffin." Makes 12 muffins.

> 1 cup oats (quick-cooking or old-fashioned)
> 1 cup vanilla yogurt
> ½ cup vegetable oil
> ¾ cup brown sugar
> 1 egg
> 1 cup flour
> ¾ teaspoon salt
> ½ teaspoon baking soda
> 1 teaspoon baking powder
> ½ cup craisins (dried cranberries)
>   powdered sugar

- Preheat oven to 400 degrees.
- Lightly grease muffin cups.
- In a large bowl, soak oats in yogurt for 5 minutes. Add oil, brown sugar, and egg, and beat well.
- In a medium bowl, sift together flour, salt, baking soda, and baking powder. Add to the oat mixture in the large bowl. Fold in craisins.
- Fill greased muffin tins and bake at 400 degrees for 20 minutes. Sprinkle with powdered sugar before serving.

The Buttonwood Inn

*O*riginally constructed as a four-room Cape Cod–style farm house in 1820, the Buttonwood Inn is today a nine-guestroom bed-and-breakfast. Innkeepers Peter and Claudia Needham bought the inn after a "write an essay, win an inn" contest sparked their imaginations. Ten months and thirty properties later, the Buttonwood opened its doors. Each morning a full breakfast is provided, featuring award-winning muffins and special entrées. A special treat for guests, candlelit dinners are served on Saturdays during January and February.

The Buttonwood Inn's abundant common space gives guests plenty of room to move around in, and makes it an ideal gathering place for groups of nine to twenty. From the formal dining room to the lower-level common room, the inn has a comfortable feel.

Although the inn is situated on a quiet, secluded road, North Conway's shops, restaurants, and other attractions remain convenient. In the summer, guests can stroll the inn's five acres of lawns and award-winning gardens, and enjoy the large in-ground swimming pool, Adirondack chairs, badminton, and horseshoes. Hiking trails go right off the back of the property. In the winter, those same hiking trails connect to 65 kilometers of groomed cross-country ski trails, part of a system of ski trails in the Mt. Washington Valley area that make up the country's largest network. Other wintertime attractions include downhill skiing, snowshoeing, ice climbing, skating, and sleigh riding.

The Buttonwood Inn

P.O. Box 1817
Mt. Surprise Road
North Conway, NH 03860
603-356-2625
Fax 603-356-3140

Cranberry Orange Scones

"We serve these scones at breakfast once or twice a week and especially when we have British and other European guests," said Innkeeper Claudia Needham. "The scones have always been well received. The trick with this recipe is to make the scones fatter than skinnier and to follow the recipe pretty closely." Makes 16 scones.

  ½ cup cranberries, chopped
  2 tablespoons sugar
  1 teaspoon orange zest
 1¼ cups flour
 1¼ cups quick-cooking oats
  ¼ cup whole-wheat flour
  1 tablespoon baking powder
  ⅛ teaspoon salt
  3 tablespoons sugar
  ¼ cup plus 2 tablespoons skim milk
  ¼ cup margarine, melted
  1 egg, beaten
  2 teaspoons sugar
  ¼ teaspoon ground cinnamon

- The night before, chop the cranberries in a food processor. Mix the cranberries with the 2 tablespoons sugar and the orange zest. Refrigerate.
- In the morning, preheat the oven to 375 degrees.
- Combine the flour, oats, whole-wheat flour, baking powder, salt, and sugar with the cranberries. Stir well.
- Combine the skim milk, margarine, and egg. Add to the flour mixture, stirring with a fork just until dry ingredients are moistened. (Dough will be stiff and sticky.)
- Turn dough out onto a sheet of waxed paper, and knead lightly 4 to 5 times. Roll dough to an 8-inch circle.
- Combine 2 teaspoons sugar and cinnamon; sprinkle over dough. Cut dough into 16 wedges with a sharp knife. Place on an ungreased cookie sheet.
- Bake in a preheated oven at 375 degrees for 10 minutes or until golden brown.

The Inn at Ludington

*I*nnkeeper Diane Shields knew many innkeepers and their inns before she entered into the business herself. She owned and operated a reservation service, and she first saw the 1889 Queen Anne Victorian mansion when she came to visit innkeepers in Ludington.

"When I found out it was for sale, I decided to pursue my dream of full-time innkeeping, and within three months had moved in, lock, stock, and barrel." The three-story home has six guestrooms, to which Diane added bathrooms and redecorated after purchasing the inn in 1990.

Guests at the inn can explore the area beaches, golf courses, or hop on the Lake Michigan car ferry. Or they might enjoy relaxing, reading, talking, or playing board games by the fireplace in the spacious parlor. Diane's homemade breakfast is served in the formal dining room, but is an informal, fun affair.

In addition to innkeeping, Diane conducts seminars for aspiring innkeepers, and writes regularly for bed-and-breakfast newsletters and magazines. She is a columnist for *The Inn Times*.

The Inn at Ludington
701 East Ludington Avenue
Ludington, MI 49431
616-845-7055

Date Bran Muffins

This recipe, with its hint of orange, has been requested again and again by repeat guests. Because the batter can be made the night before, Innkeeper Diane Shields likes these muffins as much as her guests do! Makes 2 dozen muffins.

2½ cups flour
1 cup wheat bran
⅔ cup sugar
2½ teaspoons baking soda
2 eggs
1½ cups buttermilk
½ cup oil
½ cup orange juice concentrate
1 cup pitted dates, chopped

- Preheat oven to 350 degrees.
- Place flour, wheat bran, sugar, and baking soda in a large mixing bowl.
- In a small bowl, mix eggs, buttermilk, oil, and orange juice concentrate. Add to the flour mixture and mix well.
- Fold in chopped dates. The batter will keep in the refrigerator, covered, overnight.
- Bake at 350 degrees for 20 minutes.

Stonecrest Farm
Bed & Breakfast

*S*ituated on two acres with handsome red barns and lovely old trees, Stonecrest Farm was founded as a dairy farm in 1810 and owned by the Stone family until 1967. Although the farm ceased operation about mid-century, Arthur Stone, an engineer and prominent local citizen, entertained guests such as President Calvin Coolidge and Amelia Earhart in this spacious private home.

Located 3.7 miles south of Dartmouth College in the small village of Wilder, Vermont, near the Connecticut River, Stonecrest Farm is within an easy drive of several major ski and recreation areas. While the majority of Stonecrest's guests are Dartmouth parents, alumni, and visitors, Innkeeper Gail Sanderson welcomes vacationers and businesspeople from many states and foreign countries.

A large formal living room, with a beamed ceiling and a curved staircase, features a wood stove to ward off cold nights. In warmer weather, French doors open to a private stone terrace surrounded by flowers. Stonecrest offers six guestrooms, most with queen beds, down comforters, quilts, abundant books, antiques throughout, and a baby grand piano in the living room.

The varied breakfast menu might offer fresh fruit, juice, homemade breads, muffins or scones, vegetable fritatta, orange French toast, berry pancakes with Vermont maple syrup, or a ricotta- and herb-filled omelet with red pepper sauce.

Stonecrest Farm
Bed & Breakfast
P.O. Box 504
Wilder, VT 05088
802-296-2425
Fax 802-295-1135

Gingered Lemon Wild Blueberry Muffins

Nothing beats wild blueberries, but Innkeeper Gail Sanderson has improved on wild blueberry muffins in this lemon and double-ginger version. Guests at Stonecrest Farm would inhale them if she made them any smaller. Makes 36 muffins.

    6 cups cake flour
    2 tablespoons baking powder
    2 teaspoons baking soda
    1 teaspoon ground ginger
    ½ teaspoon salt
  1 ½ cups sugar
    6 eggs
    ½ cup canola oil
    2 cups 1 percent buttermilk
    4 cups wild blueberries
    ½ cup crystallized ginger, chopped
    2 tablespoons lemon zest, finely chopped
    ⅓ cup sugar
       nonstick cooking spray

- Preheat oven to 400 degrees, or a convection oven to 375 degrees.
- Spray muffin cups with nonstick cooking spray.
- In a bowl, sift together flour, baking powder, baking soda, ginger, and salt. Set aside.
- In another bowl, beat together sugar, eggs, oil, and buttermilk. Add the buttermilk mixture to the flour mixture and stir just to blend.
- Fold in blueberries, crystallized ginger, and lemon zest.
- Place ¼ cup batter in each muffin tin and sprinkle each with ½ teaspoon sugar.
- Bake muffins for 20 to 22 minutes or until firm to the touch. Cool muffins slightly before serving.

White Swan Guest House

*P*eter Goldfarb, a transplanted Manhattanite and interior designer and contractor, found this 1898 farmhouse in 1986 while exploring the Skagit River Valley near Washington's North Cascades. Using historical photos as guides, he undertook restoration himself, redoing it from the ground up — literally. The old farmhouse, built by a Scandinavian farmer, was sinking into the fertile farmland. The first project was to lift the house, remove the old foundation, and put in a new one.

One year later, the place was completely redone into a gorgeous Queen Anne home, plus a private guest cottage in the back of the property. Peter added an old-fashioned back porch, which guests often enjoy. That fertile farmland is now sprouting new fruit trees, berry bushes, and beautiful perennials. The house is surrounded by old English-style gardens with many places to sit and enjoy the smell of roses and views of Mt. Baker and the Olympics. Indoors, the guestrooms are warm and welcoming (and one bathroom has the most incredible mountain view you'll find in any bed-and-breakfast bathroom, anywhere — it's a pleasure to brush your teeth here!).

The Skagit River runs in front of the house, and guests enjoy walks or bike rides along it and the area country roads. In April, the famous tulips and daffodils of the LaConner area bulb farms are in full bloom, a stone's throw from the house. LaConner's restaurants, galleries, and antique shops are just six miles away. The White Swan is convenient for travelers to Seattle (to the south), Vancouver (to the north), the San Juan Islands (west), and the North Cascades National Park (east).

White Swan Guest House

1388 Moore Road
Mount Vernon, WA 98273
360-445-6805

Healthy, Spicy Oatmeal Carrot Muffins

Innkeeper Peter Goldfarb developed this recipe to offer guests a high-energy muffin that was moist and tasty, too. It's a good "pantry" recipe, using ingredients almost always on hand. Makes 12 muffins.

- 1 cup flour
- 1 cup whole-wheat flour
- 1 tablespoon baking powder
- ½ teaspoon salt
- ½ cup quick-cooking oats
- 1 teaspoon cinnamon
- 1 egg, beaten
- 1 cup milk
- 3 tablespoons molasses
- ½ cup vegetable oil
- ½ cup golden raisins
- 1 carrot, grated
- ½ cup brown sugar
  nonstick cooking spray, optional
  orange marmalade

- Preheat oven to 400 degrees.
- Line muffin pan with paper liners or spray with nonstick cooking spray.
- Sift flours, baking powder, salt, oats, and cinnamon together in a large bowl.
- In a separate bowl, mix egg, milk, molasses, oil, raisins, carrot, and brown sugar together.
- Add egg mixture to flour mixture, stirring just until all ingredients are mixed.
- Divide batter among 12 sprayed or paper-lined muffin tins.
- Bake for 15 to 20 minutes, until golden brown on top and knife comes out dry. Cool, serve with orange marmalade, and enjoy!

McGregor Manor

"*A*fter having traveled all over with my military husband and our children," said Innkeeper Carolyn Scott, "we fell in love with this old Victorian home and simply had to do something with it. Thus, McGregor Manor was born." The home was built by an early lumber baron, and the various woods used in the house reflect its heritage. A Jenny Lind–style staircase railing, tin ceilings, a recessed fireplace, oak pocket doors, stained glass windows, and beautiful arches throughout the house add much to the beauty of the house.

McGregor, a small town located right on the Mississippi River in northeast Iowa, offers hiking, fishing, snowmobiling, unique shops and antique stores, and is Carolyn's hometown. The town features two arts and crafts shows each year, and nearby are Pikes Peak State Park and Effigy Mounds National Monument.

The inn opened in July 1995, and has four guestrooms. The Scotts serve a full breakfast, afternoon tea, and evening desserts. From the spacious wrap-around porch, guests can catch glimpses of wild turkeys and a panoramic view of the surrounding hills. Eagles are plentiful on the river, and it is a thrill to watch them as they soar above the river bluffs.

McGregor Manor
P.O. Box 127, 320 Fourth Street
McGregor, IA 52157
319-873-2600
Fax 319-873-2218

Honey Citrus Oat Muffins

The glaze on these tasty muffins give them that extra sweet, tangy zip! Makes 12 muffins.

> 1 cup quick-cooking oats
> 1 8-ounce carton plain nonfat or low-fat yogurt
> ½ cup honey
> ¼ cup skim milk
> 3 tablespoons low-fat margarine
> 2 teaspoons grated lime, lemon, or orange peel
> 2 egg whites, slightly beaten
> 1½ cups flour
> 2 teaspoons baking powder
> ½ teaspoon baking soda
> ¼ teaspoon salt, optional
> nonstick cooking spray, optional

Glaze

> ¾ cup powdered sugar
> 1 teaspoon grated lime, lemon, or orange peel
> 4 teaspoons lime, lemon, or orange juice

- Preheat oven to 375 degrees.
- Line muffin pan with paper liners or spray bottoms only with nonstick cooking spray.
- In a large bowl, combine oats with yogurt, honey, milk, margarine, and citrus peel. Let stand 10 minutes. Stir in egg whites until blended.
- In a large bowl, combine flour, baking powder, baking soda, and salt. Stir in yogurt mixture until just moist. Fill muffin cups almost full.
- To make glaze, combine ingredients and mix until smooth.
- Bake 20 to 24 minutes or until light golden brown. Let muffins stand a few minutes; remove from pan. Cool slightly, then dip tops in glaze.

The Ellery House
Bed & Breakfast

*C*ooking is enjoyable for Joan and Jim Halquist, as is working on old houses, being self-employed, and offering a service people want — all important prerequisites for innkeeping. Also, "Joan and I wanted to work together in a small business" and be home for their children, Jim said.

The Halquists opened their inn in 1988, the second bed-and-breakfast in Duluth, home of the University of Minnesota at Duluth, many businesses, and the gateway to Lake Superior's North Shore. The inn is an 1890 Queen Anne Victorian, built four blocks from Lake Superior for Ellery Holliday, a local real estate tycoon. Three of the four guestrooms have lake views, and the guestrooms and common areas feature stained glass windows and antiques. The B&B is close to restaurants, downtown Canal Park, and the "lake walk" paved pathway and boardwalk that runs along the Lake Superior shoreline.

The Ellery House
Bed & Breakfast
28 South 21st Avenue East
Duluth, MN 55812
218-724-7639
Toll-free 800-355-3794

Lemon-Lovers Muffins

These yummy muffins are typical of the lower-fat treats that Joan and Jim Halquist prepare for their guests. Joan recommends that mini-muffin tins are used. "If regular muffin tins are used, the muffins will be less lemony," she comments. Makes 24 mini-muffins.

    2 cups unbleached flour
    1 teaspoon baking powder
    1 teaspoon baking soda
    ¼ cup sugar
    2 tablespoons honey
    2 eggs
 1 ¼ cups non-fat vanilla yogurt
    2 tablespoons butter or low-fat margarine, melted
    2 tablespoons canola oil
    1 tablespoon lemon zest, grated

Lemon Syrup
    ½ cup fresh lemon juice
    ⅓ cup sugar
    4 tablespoons water

- Preheat oven to 375 degrees.
- Spray muffin cups with nonstick cooking spray.
- In small bowl, stir together flour, baking powder, and baking soda.
- In another, larger bowl, combine sugar, honey, eggs, yogurt, melted butter or margarine, oil, and lemon zest. Beat well. Blend in the flour mixture.
- Fill muffin cups about ⅔ full.
- Bake 15 minutes, or until the tops are delicately browned.
- While muffins bake, prepare the syrup. Combine the lemon juice, sugar, and water in a small saucepan. Bring to a boil for 1 minute.
- When muffins are done, remove from oven and gently poke the top of each muffin 3 times with a fork. Drizzle syrup over each hot muffin. Serve warm.

Bagley House

*T*his 1772 country home is owned and operated by "the two Sues," as friends and colleagues know them: Susan Backhouse and Suzanne O'Connor. The Sues chose this country location for their inn, just a ten-minute drive from downtown Freeport, with its famous L.L. Bean headquarters store and outlet shopping. They enjoy the peace and quiet of the country but also appreciate the proximity to stores, restaurants, museums, and colleges.

The Bagley House is a Greek Revival– and Colonial–style farmhouse, now situated on six acres (which include blueberry bushes, from which many a morning meal has been made!). Furnished with antiques and featuring the original wide "pumpkin pine" floors in many rooms, the home has one guestroom downstairs and four upstairs. Originally, it was built as an inn, and now, after many years of other uses, has come full circle.

Guests can enjoy the library or gather in the kitchen around the brick fireplace and large table, chatting while breakfast is being prepared. Susan Backhouse, originally from England, often prepares authentic scones, English muffins, or other fare from old family recipes, and she willingly explains the differences from Americanized versions. Both Sues are well-versed on area activities and dining and are happy to help their guests explore the area.

Bagley House
1290 Royalsborough Road
Durham, ME 04222
207-865-6566
Fax 207-353-5878

Sourdough Whole-Wheat English Muffins

These truly are "English" muffins, prepared by native Brit Innkeeper Sue Backhouse. Sue has tended her sourdough starter carefully, and it often finds its way into waffles, pancakes, or these English muffins at the Bagley House. Makes 12 muffins.

1 cup sourdough starter
1 tablespoon active dry yeast, dissolved and proofed in ¾ cup warm water (105 to 115 degrees F.)
¾ cup whole-wheat flour
6 tablespoons yellow cornmeal
2 tablespoons powdered buttermilk
1 teaspoon salt
2 cups flour

- In a large bowl, combine starter and dissolved yeast. Mix well.
- Combine whole-wheat flour, 4 tablespoons of the cornmeal, powdered buttermilk, and salt. Add to liquid, mixing well until stiff.
- Add remaining 2 cups of flour, turn out on lightly floured board, and knead until smooth and elastic. Adding flour is necessary to prevent sticking. Cover with inverted bowl. Allow to rest 10 minutes.
- Roll dough to ¾-inch thickness. Using a empty, cleaned tuna can or a 4-inch cutter, cut dough into muffins. Dip muffins in additional 2 tablespoons of cornmeal to coat both sides.
- Place on ungreased cookie sheet and leave in a warm place to rise until doubled in size (35 to 45 minutes).
- Meanwhile, preheat electric griddle to 275 degrees.
- Using a spatula, lay muffins carefully on the griddle, and cook for a total of 25 minutes, turning every 5 minutes — 5 minutes on one side, then flipping to cook for 5 minutes on the other side, then flipping again, etc. Cool on a wire rack.

The Inn at 410 Bed & Breakfast

"*T*he place with the personal touch," the Inn at 410 offers four seasons of hospitality. A scrumptious gourmet breakfast is served in Innkeepers Howard and Sally Krueger's dining room each morning; the aroma of home-baked cookies greets guests at the end of their daily excursions.

Ideally located just blocks from historic downtown Flagstaff, the Inn at 410 can serve as a home base for a northern Arizona getaway. Many restaurants, cafes, shops, and galleries are within walking distance of the inn. Day trip destinations from the inn include Grand Canyon National Park, Sedona and Oak Creek Canyon, and the Painted Desert and Petrified Forest.

The inn has nine distinctive suites. Several have private entrances, fireplaces, or whirlpools. One suite is accessible to wheelchairs.

In the dining room, guests are served a full breakfast that features low-fat, low-cholesterol recipes. The inn's spacious parlor, trimmed with oak and furnished with antiques, is a relaxing place to sip hot cider and curl up with a book in front of the fireplace. The gazebo, surrounded by perennial gardens, offers summer guests an intimate retreat for afternoon iced tea.

The Inn at 410 Bed & Breakfast
410 North Leroux Street
Flagstaff, AZ 86001
520-774-0088
Toll-free 800-744-2008

Sweet Potato Molasses Muffins

The natural sweetness of the potatoes themselves is all the "sugar" this recipe needs.
Makes 12 muffins.

1¼ cups flour
½ cup whole-wheat flour
2 teaspoons baking powder
1 teaspoon cinnamon
½ teaspoon ground ginger
½ teaspoon salt
1 large orange-fleshed sweet potato, baked until tender, peeled, and puréed in food processor
½ cup skim milk
½ cup unsulphured light molasses
2 eggs, lightly beaten
3 tablespoons margarine, melted
   nonstick cooking spray

- Preheat oven to 400 degrees.
- Spray 12 muffin cups with nonstick cooking spray.
- Measure flours, baking powder, cinnamon, ginger, and salt into a large bowl. Stir to combine thoroughly. Set aside.
- In a medium bowl, whisk together puréed sweet potato, skim milk, molasses, eggs, and melted margarine.
- Add the flour mixture to the sweet potato mixture and stir by hand just until blended. Do not over mix.
- Use an ice cream scoop to fill prepared muffin cups. Bake for 25 minutes or until toothpick inserted into the center of a muffin comes out clean. Cool in pan 5 minutes, then turn onto wire rack.

The Half Penney Inn
Bed & Breakfast

*I*f your idea of an ideal trip to Vermont includes staying at a historic country inn along a quiet, unpaved road, then the Half Penney Inn should be on your itinerary.

Surrounded by meadows and woods, the Half Penney boasts that the Appalachian Trail runs right behind the inn. Guests can bike the scenic White River Valley, or kayak, tube, canoe, fish, and swim in the White River. Cross-country skiing begins out the door, and major alpine ski areas are a short drive away. The inn's dog, Cody, guides guests to the nearby beaver pond (and asks only that a stick be thrown in return).

The inn, built by Levi Hazen in 1775, is named after the Hazen livestock brand, a half penney. The original home was a two-story log cabin, where the Hazens raised 13 children in two rooms. In 1803 a brick house was added, with bricks fired right on site. Gretchen and Bob Fairweather opened this inn in 1991, something Gretchen wanted to do since she was 12 years old. Before innkeeping, Gretchen managed a local radio station, and now she adds freelance naturalist/trail guide to her duties at the inn; Bob continues to work at a local medical center.

The Half Penney Inn
Bed & Breakfast
Box 84, Handy Road
West Hartford, VT 05084
802-295-6082

Versatile Yogurt Muffins

"This is a wonderful, moist, versatile muffin," said Innkeeper Gretchen Fairweather, "and they freeze well. We use all the combinations (below), depending on the season. Do not try blueberry or mixed berry yogurts," she warns. "The muffins taste fine, but come out of the oven an unappetizing gray color." Makes 12 muffins.

      2 cups flour
     ⅔ cup sugar
      1 teaspoon baking powder
      1 teaspoon baking soda
     ¼ cup vegetable oil
      1 egg
      1 8-ounce carton of yogurt (see below)
      2 cups fruit (see below)
         nonstick cooking spray

Yogurt and Fruit Combinations
- lemon yogurt and blueberries (fresh or frozen; if frozen, do not thaw before baking)
- peach yogurt and fresh peaches or nectarines, peeled and cubed
- strawberry yogurt and 1 cup stewed rhubarb
- cappuccino yogurt and hazelnuts, chopped
- vanilla yogurt and strawberries, sliced

- Preheat oven to 400 degrees.
- Spray muffin cups with nonstick cooking spray.
- Mix flour, sugar, baking powder, and baking soda in a large bowl.
- In a separate bowl, mix oil, egg, and yogurt.
- Stir in flour mixture, then fold in 2 cups of fruit.
- Spoon into muffin tins, and bake in 400-degree oven for 20 to 25 minutes. Cool in tin for 5 minutes, then remove to complete cooling.

The Half Penney Inn
Bed & Breakfast

*I*f your idea of an ideal trip to Vermont includes staying at a historic country inn along a quiet, unpaved road, then the Half Penney Inn should be on your itinerary.

Surrounded by meadows and woods, the Half Penney boasts that the Appalachian Trail runs right behind the inn. Guests can bike the scenic White River Valley, or kayak, tube, canoe, fish, and swim in the White River. Cross-country skiing begins out the door, and major alpine ski areas are a short drive away. The inn's dog, Cody, guides guests to the nearby beaver pond (and asks only that a stick be thrown in return).

The inn, built by Levi Hazen in 1775, is named after the Hazen livestock brand, a half penney. The original home was a two-story log cabin, where the Hazens raised 13 children in two rooms. In 1803 a brick house was added, with bricks fired right on site. Gretchen and Bob Fairweather opened this inn in 1991, something Gretchen wanted to do since she was 12 years old. Before innkeeping, Gretchen managed a local radio station, and now she adds freelance naturalist/trail guide to her duties at the inn; Bob continues to work at a local medical center.

The Half Penney Inn
Bed & Breakfast
Box 84, Handy Road
West Hartford, VT 05084
802-295-6082

Apricot Butter

"Guests love this as an alternative to butter or margarine on toast or English muffins," *notes Gretchen Fairweather. "It has a nice sweet-tart wake-up taste. I put it in pretty* *custard cups so it is all ready to go on the breakfast table. This keeps well, but it never* *lasts very long once guests get a taste of it!" Makes approximately 2 ⅓ cups.*

> 2 cups fresh apricots, peeled and cut up
> ¼ cup orange juice
> 2 tablespoons honey

- Cut up the apricots with kitchen scissors. If the apricots are small, cut them into quarters; if large, eighths.
- Put apricots and orange juice in a saucepan. Cook over medium heat, stirring until apricots are soft and orange juice is absorbed. "You may need to add a little more juice if the liquid is absorbed before the apricots are a spreadable consistency."
- Remove from heat, and stir in the honey. Store, covered, in the refrigerator. Serve cold.

Wedgwood Inns

*W*hen Carl Glassman and Dinie Silnutzer-Glassman decided to make career changes, they did their research, worked in the hospitality industry, and then threw caution to the wind. A nineteenth-century home came up for sale, one that Carl had noticed for quite some time, and they started in on the major restoration needed.

The resulting Wedgwood House, named after their collection of china, opened in 1982, just a few blocks from the village center of this historic Bucks County river town. But that was just the beginning — it turned out they enjoyed innkeeping so much, they restored other inns, and now teach classes to aspiring innkeepers, as well.

Their bed-and-breakfasts are nineteenth-century homes on more than two acres of landscaped grounds. Guests can enjoy the gardens, gazebo, and a game of croquet, played in traditional costume, at tea-time in the summer. In the winter, tea and treats are enjoyed fireside in the parlor.

Dinie and Carl offer fresh-baked pastries, warm comforters, a glass of homemade almond liqueur before bed, and other touches to make guests comfortable. They host a number of special events, including historic reenactments, romantic getaways, relaxation retreats and other events created purely for guests' enjoyment.

Wedgwood Inns
111 West Bridge Street
New Hope, PA 18938
215-862-2520
Fax 215-862-2570

Fresh Fruit Shortcakes

"Fresh is best" is the motto at the Wedgwood's kitchen. Nadine "Dinie" Silnutzer-Glassman also insists that low-fat and healthy recipes must taste good. She developed this breakfast treat with just those two points in mind. Makes 16 shortcakes.

 $\frac{1}{2}$ cup sugar
 1 teaspoon cinnamon
 1 cup unbleached flour
 1 cup whole-wheat flour
 1 tablespoon baking powder
 $\frac{1}{3}$ cup canola oil
 $\frac{2}{3}$ cup skim milk
 4 cups fresh peaches, strawberries, or other fruit, chopped and lightly sugared
 1 cup low-fat vanilla yogurt

- Preheat oven to 375.
- Mix 1 tablespoon of the sugar with $\frac{1}{2}$ teaspoon of the cinnamon in a small bowl. Set aside to use as a topping.
- In another bowl, combine the remaining sugar, the remaining $\frac{1}{2}$ teaspoon cinnamon, the flours, and the baking powder.
- Combine oil and milk; stir oil mixture into flour mixture until it can be formed into a ball.
- Drop by tablespoons onto an ungreased baking sheet and flatten. Sprinkle with the cinnamon-sugar topping. Bake 10 to 12 minutes.
- To serve, place hot shortcakes on each plate. Spoon fresh fruit onto each shortcake, and top with a dollop of vanilla yogurt.

The Inn on South Street

*G*uests of this stately two-hundred-year-old mansion might enjoy this breakfast beverage in the second-floor country kitchen, overlooking the river and the ocean. Breakfast is made and served there by Eva and Jack Downs, who turned their spacious home into an inn after their children had been raised here.

Eva, formerly an occupational therapist and child care administrator, and Jack, an American history professor, love treating guests to their home and town. Built in the Greek Revival style, the home was moved long ago to this location by a team of oxen. After completely redecorating their home of almost thirty years, the Downses opened four guestrooms, one of which is an apartment suite. The herb and "secret" gardens are exquisite and worth a visit by guests.

The inn is located in Kennebunkport's quiet historic area and is listed on the National Register of Historic Places. Guests can walk down tree-lined streets to restaurants, shops, and the ocean, or take a short drive to golf courses, tennis courts, nature preserves, and wonderful beaches.

The Inn on South Street
P.O. Box 478A
Kennebunkport, ME 04046
207-967-5151
Toll-free 800-963-5151

Herbed Yogurt Cheese

This spicy spread always gets the "thumbs up" from Eva and Jack Downs' guests, who enjoy it on crackers or breads as part of afternoon refreshments. Makes about two cups.

> yogurt cheese from 1 quart of plain low-fat yogurt (see below)
> 1 tablespoon fresh basil leaves, chopped, or dried basil
> 1 teaspoon lemon juice
> 1 teaspoon salt
> 1 clove fresh garlic, minced
> 1 teaspoon dill weed, chopped, or dried dill
> ½ teaspoon dried tarragon, ground

- To make yogurt cheese, place 1 quart of plain low-fat yogurt (without gelatin) in a sieve or a Melitta®-brand coffee cone lined with a paper coffee filter. Let drain in the refrigerator about 6 to 8 hours until the yogurt is solid and the whey is drained off.
- Mix yogurt cheese with basil, lemon juice, salt, garlic, dill weed, and tarragon, and let stand 2 hours before serving. Serve with favorite breads and crackers. Store, covered, in refrigerator.

The Weare-House
Bed & Breakfast

*L*ocated in Weare, New Hampshire, the Weare-House Bed-and-Breakfast is a delightful country farmhouse with a huge barn. The main house was built in 1819 and features original wide pine floors, hand-hewn beams, and low windows that overlook surrounding pastures and hills. The four guestrooms are furnished with antique pieces and cozy beds with lofty goose down comforters. The living room has a charming fireplace. Guests are welcome to relax in this room with a book or current magazine left for your enjoyment. Children will enjoy the toys and games that are available. The house, barn, and 12 acres of land are available for guests to enjoy.

Ellen and Curt Goldsberry, high school sweethearts from Ohio, left a Boston suburb to open their B&B in 1993. At the time, their son Nathan was two, and they opted to enjoy all the activities and advantages of living in New Hampshire full-time.

Children and animal-lovers always enjoy a visit to the Weare-House barn. It's where two miniature Sicilian donkeys, horses, and laying hens reside. The hens contribute fresh eggs to the hearty, country breakfast, served with fresh fruit and homemade goods baked each day.

The Weare-House
Bed & Breakfast
76 Quaker Street
Weare, NH 03281
603-529-2660

Lower-Fat Granola

Innkeeper Ellen Goldsberry experimented with a number of granola recipes to find a lower-fat version (not easy!) that was simple and delicious. This is the result, and "many guests find it so tempting they have it in addition to the main entrée, which we take as a great compliment," she said. Makes 12 servings.

6 cups old-fashioned rolled oats
½ cup slivered almonds
¼ cup canola oil
½ cup honey
½ cup molasses
1 cup water
¼ brown sugar
1 cup raisins

■ Preheat oven to 350 degrees.
■ Mix oats and almonds in a large bowl.
■ Heat canola oil, honey, molasses, water, and brown sugar, stirring until it comes to a low boil. Pour hot liquid over oats and almonds, and mix.
■ Bake on baking sheet at 350 degrees for 35 minutes, stirring frequently. Add raisins when granola has cooled; store in airtight container.

The Inn at the Round Barn Farm

*I*n the heart of Vermont amidst 85 acres of mountains, meadows, and ponds is the Inn at the Round Barn Farm, which gets its name from the 12-sided barn built in 1910 and now fully restored. Until the 1960s, this was a working dairy farm. Then, Jack and Doreen Simko and their daughter AnneMarie DeFreest converted the nineteenth-century farmhouse and attached horse barn to guestrooms, common spaces, and a cross-country ski center. The round barn is now used for large gatherings, and in the lower level is a sixty-foot indoor lap pool that extends into a greenhouse.

The inn offers 11 guestrooms, all with original pine floors. The first floor includes a library with a wood-burning fireplace, a good selection of coffeetable books about Vermont, and a decanter of sherry. In the lower level is a game room with an antique pool table, an organ, and many modern-day diversions such as a VCR. Breakfast, served in a sunny room with a view of the hills, includes juice, fresh fruit, muffins, and a daily hot entrée.

The inn has thirty kilometers of groomed cross-country ski trails and offers guests rentals — including snowshoe rentals. In the wintertime, downhill skiing is just a few minutes away, and the inn is beautifully decorated and lit for the holidays. In the summertime, the inn hosts concerts and art exhibits, and is an ideal gathering place for large groups.

The Inn at the Round Barn Farm

R.R. Box 247
East Warren Road
Waitsfield, VT 05673
802-496-2276
Fax 802-496-8832

Vermont Maple Sausage Patties

A "from scratch" breakfast may extend all the way to the sausage at the Inn at the Round Barn Farm. This is a rare low-fat version of pork sausage, featuring a hint of pure Vermont maple syrup. Makes 16 patties.

- 2 slices whole-wheat bread
- ⅓ cup low-fat milk
- 1 pound pork tenderloin, trimmed of fat
- 1 cup peeled, grated apple (about 1 large apple)
- 2 tablespoons pure Vermont maple syrup
- 1 teaspoon dried rubbed sage
- 1 teaspoon dried thyme leaves
- 1 teaspoon salt
- ½ teaspoon freshly ground black pepper
- ½ teaspoon ground ginger
- ½ teaspoon ground mace
  - pinch of ground red pepper (cayenne)

- ■ Finely crumble bread into a mixing bowl, stir in milk, and set aside to soak.
- ■ Finely chop the pork with a large knife. Add the chopped pork to the soaked bread along with apples, maple syrup, sage, thyme, salt, black pepper, ginger, mace, and red pepper.
- ■ Mix together thoroughly with clean hands. (The mixture will be fairly soft.) Form the sausage mixture into 16 patties, using about 3 tablespoons per patty. (Wash hands and everything touched by raw pork thoroughly.)
- ■ Heat a large nonstick skillet over medium-low heat. Brown half of the patties until no longer pink in the center, 3 to 4 minutes per side. Transfer to a serving plate and cover to keep warm. Repeat with remaining patties.
- ■ Patties can also be baked in the oven at 400 degrees for 5 to 8 minutes. This keeps more of the flavor in the sausage.

ARIZONA

Inn at 410 Bed & Breakfast, The; Flagstaff, AZ —
Apricot-Almond Couscous (47), Sweet Potato Molasses Muffins (113), Yogurt Parfait (37)
Peppertrees Bed & Breakfast Inn; Tucson, AZ — *Popover Fruit Pie (35)*

CALIFORNIA

Beazley House Bed & Breakfast Inn, The; Napa, CA —
Chili-Cheese Puff (53), Creme Caramel Overnight French Toast (55), Pineapple Bread (91)
Healdsburg Inn on the Plaza; Healdsburg, CA — *Autumn Fruit Compote (15)*
Howard Creek Ranch Inn; Westport, CA — *Baked Apples with Granola (19)*
Lord Mayor's Bed & Breakfast Inn; Long Beach, CA — *Mango Delight (27)*

FLORIDA

Clauser's Bed & Breakfast; Lake Helen, FL — *Applesauce Oatmeal Muffins (93)*

IOWA

McGregor Manor; McGregor, IA — *Honey Citrus Oat Muffins (107)*

MAINE

Bagley House; Durham, ME — *Sourdough Whole-Wheat English Muffins (111)*
Blue Harbor House; Camden, ME — *Blueberry Stuffed French Toast (51)*
Inn on South Street, The; Kennebunkport, ME — *Minted Watermelon Refresher (11),*
Herbed Yogurt Cheese (121)

MASSACHUSSETS

Inn at One Main Street, The; Falmouth, MA — *Gingerbread Pancakes (61)*

MICHIGAN

Big Bay Point Lighthouse Bed & Breakfast; Big Bay, MI — *Apple Pancakes (43)*
Garden Grove Bed & Breakfast; Union Pier, MI —
Luscious Lemon Pancakes with Blueberry Sauce (69)
Inn at Ludington, The; Ludington, MI — *Date Bran Muffins (101)*
Parsonage 1908, The; Holland, MI — *Honey Baked Apples (25)*
Pentwater Inn, The; Pentwater, MI — *Baked Omelet Extraordinaire (49),*
Tart Cherry Crepes (77)

MINNESOTA

Ellery House Bed & Breakfast, The; Duluth, MN — *Lemon-Lovers Muffins (109)*
Park Row Bed & Breakfast; St. Peter, MN — *Minnesota Wild Rice Pancakes (71)*
Desoto at Prior's; St. Paul, MN — *Blueberry Muffins (95)*

NEW HAMPSHIRE

Apple Gate Bed & Breakfast; Peterborough, NH — *Peach Melba (29)*
Bernerhof Inn, The; Glen, NH — *Cantaloupe Cooler (7)*
Buttonwood Inn, The; North Conway, NH — *Cranberry Orange Scones (99)*
Inn at Maplewood Farm, The; Hillsborough, NH — *Chilled Cantaloupe Soup (21),*
Poached Pears (31)
Rosewood Country Inn, The; Bradford, NH — *Citrus Frost & Tropical Blend (9)*
Weare-House Bed & Breakfast, The; Weare, NH — *Lower-Fat Granola (123)*

NEW JERSEY

Queen Victoria Bed & Breakfast Country Inn, The; Cape May, NJ —
Applesauce Bread Pudding (45)

NEW MEXICO

Grant Corner Inn; Santa Fe, NM — *Kewpie's Baked Eggs with Shrimp (67),*
Raspberry Fizz (13)
Inn on the Rio; Taos, NM — *Southwest Bake (75)*

NORTH CAROLINA

Mast Farm Inn; Valle Crucis, NC — *Three-Grain Pancakes (79)*
Waverly Inn, The; Hendersonville, NC — *John's Buckwheat Pancakes (65)*

OREGON

Pine Meadow Inn; Merlin (Grant's Pass), OR — *Fresh Veggie Frittata (59),*
Granny Smith Oatmeal Waffles (63)

PENNSYLVANIA

Wedgwood Inns; New Hope, PA — *Apple Dutch Babies (39), Fresh Fruit Shortcakes (119)*

TEXAS

Ant Street Inn, The; Brenham, TX — *Tejas Breakfast Cups (81)*
McCallum House, The; Austin, TX — *Blueberry Gingerbread with Lemon Curd (85)*
Yellow Rose – a Bed & Breakfast; San Antonio, TX — *Fat-Free Omelet (57)*

VERMONT

Governor's Inn, The; Ludlow, VT — *Grandmother's Graham Bread (89)*
Half Penney Inn Bed & Breakfast, The; West Hartford, VT —
Apricot Butter (117), Versatile Yogurt Muffins (115)
Inn at the Round Barn Farm, The; Waitsfield, VT — *Vermont Maple Sausage Patties (125)*
Stonecrest Farm Bed & Breakfast; Wilder, VT —
Fruit Kabobs with Lemon Ginger Cream (23), Gingered Lemon Wild Blueberry Muffins (103)

VIRGINIA

Hidden Inn, The; Orange, VA — *Poached Winter Fruit (33)*
Lynchburg Mansion Inn Bed & Breakfast, The; Lynchburg, VA —
Quick and Easy Vegetarian Frittata (73)
Owl and the Pussycat Bed & Breakfast, The; Petersburg, VA — *Fruited Bran Bread (87)*

WASHINGTON

Salisbury House; Seattle, WA — *Apple Coffeecake (83)*
White Swan Guest House; Mount Vernon, WA — *Healthy, Spicy Oatmeal Carrot Muffins*
(105)

WISCONSIN

Stout Trout Bed & Breakfast, The; Springbrook, WI — *Apple Oatmeal Pancakes (41)*
Thimbleberry Inn Bed & Breakfast; Bayfield, WI — *Craisin Yogurt Muffins (97)*

WYOMING

Window on the Winds Bed & Breakfast; Pinedale, WY — *Baked Apples (17)*

Ordering Information

Order additional copies of any of our popular B&B cookbook editions from your bookstore, gift shop, or by mail.

Innkeepers' Best Muffins *and* **Innkeepers' Best Low-Fat Breakfast Recipes** *are the first in a series of practical one-topic cookbooks showcasing bed-and-breakfast innkeepers' outstanding recipes. Each 6 x 9–inch paperback retails for $9.95 ($12.95 each by 4th class mail; $13.95 each UPS ground service).*

WAKE UP & SMELL THE COFFEE *is a series of hefty 8 ½ x 11–inch softcover cookbooks that feature travel information, maps, an index, as well as more than ten chapters of breakfast, brunch, and other favorite fare from B&Bs in a particular region.*

> **Lake States Edition** *has 203 recipes from 125 B&Bs in Michigan, Wisconsin, and Michigan: $15.95 ($18.95 by 4th class mail; $19.95 UPS ground service).*
> **Southwest Edition** *boasts more than 170 recipes from 65 B&Bs in Texas, Arizona, and New Mexico: $14.95 ($17.95 each by 4th class mail, $18.95 each sent UPS).*
> **Pacific Northwest Edition** *features more than 130 recipes from 58 B&Bs in Washington and Oregon: $11.95 ($14.95 each by 4th class mail, $15.95 each sent UPS).*

Look for **WAKE UP & SMELL THE COFFEE's Northern New England Edition** *(Maine, Vermont, and New Hampshire), and* **Chocolate for Breakfast and Tea,** *coming soon!*

TO ORDER BY MAIL, send a check to Down to Earth Publications, 1032 W. Montana, St. Paul, MN 55117. Make checks payable to Down to Earth Publications. MN residents please add 7% sales tax. **TO ORDER WITH VISA OR MASTERCARD,** call us at 800-585-6211.

Mail to: Down to Earth Publications, 1032 W. Montana, St. Paul, MN 55117.

Please send me:

> _____ *Innkeepers' Best* **Muffins**
> _____ *Innkeepers' Best* **Low-Fat Breakfasts**
> _____ *WAKE UP & SMELL THE COFFEE —* **Pacific Northwest Edition**
> _____ *WAKE UP & SMELL THE COFFEE —* **Lake States Edition**
> _____ *WAKE UP & SMELL THE COFFEE —* **Southwest Edition**

I have enclosed $_____ for _____ book(s). Send it/them to (no P.O. boxes for UPS):

Name: _____

Street: _____ Apt. No. _____

City: _____ State: _____ Zip: _____
   (Please note: No P.O. Boxes for UPS delivery)